ADVANCES IN
CRIMINOLOGICAL THEORY

ADVANCES IN CRIMINOLOGICAL THEORY

Volume Two

Edited by

William S. Laufer
and
Freda Adler

Transaction Publishers
New Brunswick (U.S.A.) and London (U.K.)

Library of Congress Catalog Number: 89-641309
ISBN: 0-88738-287-8
Printed in the United States of America

To Don Cressey

Contents

List of Tables and Figures

Tables

Figure

Foreword

Lloyd E. Ohlin

I was especially pleased to learn that the editors of *Advances in Criminological Theory* were planning to dedicate the second volume of their new serial to the late Professor Donald R. Cressey and equally pleased to be asked to prepare this foreword. There are many reasons why this dedication to Don Cressey constitutes such an apt choice. The new work ranges widely in its coverage of theoretical developments in crimonology and criminal justice, and so did the theoretical inquiries by Cressey. He is perhaps most noted for his espousal, development, and defense of the theory of differential association by Edwin Sutherland, and his demonstration of the utility of the theory in practice as it applied to changing criminals, rehabilitating drug addicts, and understanding compulsive crimes. However, he made important theoretical contributions on a number of criminological and criminal justice issues quite apart from the matter of delinquency causation.

For his doctoral dissertation he undertook a study of white-collar offenders involved in violations of trust, most notably embezzlers. He interviewed offenders in great depth in the Illinois state prison system and the federal prison at Terre Haute. Utilizing the method of analytic induction, he searched for a generalizable explanation of their conduct and found it in the existence of a perceived unshareable problem, to which the embezzlement offered a temporary solution. The cognitive structure of the embezzler also required the resort to rationalizations (e.g., I was only borrowing) to protect his conventional self-concept. This theoretical construction appeared in *Other People's Money* in 1953. More recently, Cressey returned to the study of white-collar crime with a focus on corporation codes of ethical conduct. His renewed interest in this subject appears in his essay in the first volume of this book under the title "The Poverty of Theory in Corporate Crime Research," the publication of which appeared after his death.

Cressey also made major theoretical contributions to our understanding of the organizational dynamics of prison life. In a series of articles in the late 1950s and early 1960s, he analyzed the social organization of the prison and the interactive adjustments of both staff and inmates to prison conditions and role definitions. One of his most frequently cited and reprinted articles concerned a theoretical exploration of the effect of contradictory directives in a complex organization such as the prison.

This interest in the organizational aspects of crime and criminal justice found perhaps its clearest expression in his study of organized crime for the President's Commission on Law Enforcement and the Administration of Justice in 1965–1967. He was concerned with the development of a theory of the structure and function of organized crime and its emergence as a social system. His access to the U.S. Department of Justice and FBI files and wire tap data provided a rich source for tracing organized crime connections, the results of which appeared in 1969 in his book, *Theft of a Nation: The Structure and Operations of Organized Crime in America*.

Finally, it should be noted that Donald Cressey was always interested in understanding more about the functioning of legal process in the criminal justice system. This interest gained its most visible form in an exploration of the plea bargaining process, a study he undertook with Professor Arthur I. Rosett of the law faculty of the University of California, Los Angeles. This study resulted in 1976 in a widely quoted book entitled, *Justice By Consent: Plea Bargains in the American Courthouse*.

These major publications reflect the breadth of Donald Cressey's wide-ranging search for theoretical understanding of many aspects of crime and criminal justice. He loved to think and write about these matters and did so in a great number of articles that explored and elaborated on other themes and issues as well. Invariably he approached these topics from a sociological concern with organizational structure and function or a social psychological interest in the cognitive processes of offenders. The field of criminology has profited greatly from his many theoretical and empirical contributions. No one touching the subjects he addressed could fail to take account of those contributions in building on his insights or taking off in new directions.

1

Whose Prophet Is Cesare Beccaria? An Essay on the Origins of Criminological Theory

G. O. W. Mueller

Cesare Bonesana, Marchese de Beccaria, known as Cesare Beccaria, was born on March 15, 1738, in Milan, Italy. Educated as an economist, tutored in liberal circles, he published a remarkable essay when only 26 years old: the *Essay on Crimes and Punishments*.[1] Nothing else was remarkable about the life of Beccaria. But that essay shook the then-extant criminal justice system and has had an impact on criminological theory ever since. The essay was an indictment of the brutal, inhumane manner in which all European jurisdictions then dealt with the crime problem, and it affected criminological theory development for two centuries. In this essay I shall deal with the contemporary social significance of Beccaria's criminal policy, its influence on criminological theory, and its practical global impact.

Beccaria made a significant impression on the founders of the American republic. The first American edition of the *Essay on Crimes and Punishments* was published in New York in 1773, just three years before the American Declaration of Independence. Three of the founding fathers of the United States were ardent admirers of Beccaria—Benjamin Franklin, John Adams, and Thomas Jefferson, principal author of the Declaration of Independence. About Adams, Thorsten Sellin reminded us: "In 1770, a young Boston lawyer, John Adams, respectfully quoted Beccaria when he addressed the jury in 'defense of the British soldiers implicated in what became known as the Boston Massacre' '' (1980:141). Jefferson, as Marvin Wolfgang noted, "knew of Beccaria and in his first inaugural address as the third president of the U.S.A., proposed what he called 'Equal and exact justice to all men.' In 1779 he drafted 'A Bill of Proportioning Crimes and Punishments' '' (1979:435). I doubt, however, that Jefferson read the *Essay on Crimes and Punishments* in its entirety, as his proposed bill contained proportionate corporal punishments which Beccaria would have condemned as unnecessarily cruel. Fortunately, Jefferson's bill never became law. It would indeed have been inconsistent with the Bill of Rights' prohibition of cruel and unusual punishments (Eighth Amendment to the U.S. Constitution) (see Morgan, 1965:248, 341, where he quotes Cotton Mather).

What do contemporary American students of criminology learn about Beccaria? An examination of nine of the leading textbooks on criminology, which, together, are read by 180,000 young men and women annually as part of their introductory instruction in criminology, reveals that all of these books discuss Beccaria. Most of them do so fairly, except one which regards Beccaria as simply the creator of a rational system designed to protect the then-new capitalist society (Quinney, 1979:5). All the others accurately stress Beccaria's principal philosophical accomplishments. One of the leading texts emphasizes his "principal application [of] the hedonistic doctrine to penology" and, thus, his insistence on deterrence (Sutherland and Cressey, 1978:56). Another likewise emphasizes Beccaria's crucial use of deterrence within hedonism, while also acknowledging his insistence on a "Just Deserts" theory, or retribution (Reid, 1985:72; 1987:58–59). A third book credits him with having founded deterrence theory and—indeed—the classical school (Haskell and Yablonski, 1983:7, 465). Yet another book finds Beccaria's principles to be three: (1) the theory of free will, (2) a society of rational human beings, and (3) hedonism (Rogers and Mays, 1987:68). A further author likewise acknowledges that Beccaria, together with Bentham, was the founder of the classical school, which he then subjects to the minor criticism of having been created by "armchair analysis and logic," rather than science (Siegel, 1983:93, 125). Authors of a somewhat radical persuasion call the *Essay* a conservative rather than a radical statement (Binder, Geis, and Bruce, 1988:103). Although it may sound conservative by today's standards, it certainly was not in 1764. Two other textbook authors, after summarizing Beccaria's principal program points, praise him for his insistence on the state's duty to ensure the protection of civil liberties (Mannle and Hirschel, 1982:30). Lastly, a Canadian scholar singles out for special mention Beccaria's identification of two main causes of crime: bad laws, and economic conditions that, according to Beccaria, explain the multitude of theft crimes among the poor (Hagan, 1985:13–14).

American criminology students on the graduate level will not only read the *Essay* itself, or the splendid Beccaria biography by Elio Monachesi (1960), but also critical analyses, such as those contained in recent articles by the American Beccaria scholar David B. Young (1983, 1987), who is particularly concerned with fathoming the inconsistencies between Beccaria's utilitarism and his retributism. All in all, Beccaria is doing well in North America, as far as the future generation of criminologists is concerned.

But to many undergraduates Beccaria will remain an enigma, especially in the current environment of changing penal philosophies—from the rehabilitative model, to a retributionist model, to an incapacitation model. The question naturally arises, just whose prophet is this mysterious philosopher Cesare Beccaria? That of the utilitarians? That of the retributists? That of the radical criminologists? That of traditional criminologists looking for causal explanations? Beccaria himself would have been astounded by this line of questioning: of course criminal law is justifiable only if it serves a purpose, namely the prevention of future crime, through deterrence and incapacitation. Said he: "The end of punishment, therefore, is no other than to prevent the criminal from doing further injury to society, and to prevent others from committing the like offense" (p. 47). To that extent, we must grant, Beccaria is a utilitarian, like his kindred in spirit Jeremy Bentham (Bentham, 1892), and scholars who espouse utilitarian notions should regard Beccaria as their prophet. Thus, James Q. Wilson, when he firmly endorsed deterrence and collective incapacitation (1975);[2] Peter Greenwood, the founder of the concept of selective incapacitation (Greenwood, 1982); and his colleage Mark Moore and associates, who further advanced the concept (Moore et al., 1985), all in effect have followed on the track marked originally by Beccaria.

But at this point Beccaria would have added that punishment must be strictly delimited so that it is proportionate to the crime committed and the harm done, in strict proportionality. Said he: "[C]rimes are only to be measured by the injury done to society" (p. 33). To that extent Beccaria is a retributionist—with one failing, I respectfully suggest: by excluding the perpetrator's criminal intention (or motivation) Beccaria violates the principle of proportionality (if not that of retribution), especially between one who steals to fend off starvation and one who steals out of greed. Nevertheless, for his basic adherence to the proportionality principle, Beccaria ought to be acclaimed by American mainstream criminologists, who have indeed returned to Beccaria's principle of punishments in proportion to the harm done,[3] following a period of disillusionment about the supposed failure of utilitarian (especially rehabilitative) models (Martinson, 1974; Lipton, Martinson, and Wilks, 1975). What contemporary American retributionists can particularly sympathize with is Beccaria's recognition of the lack of uniformity of sentences in a system of judicial discretion. Said Beccaria: "We see the same crimes punished in a different manner at different times in the same tribunals, the consequence of not having consulted the constant and invariable voice of the laws, but the erring instability of arbitrary interpretation" (p. 24).

Andrew von Hirsch, founder of the Just Deserts theory of punishment, should feel very indebted to Beccaria's lead, and indeed he recorded the indebtedness with the words: "To our surprise, we found ourselves returning to the ideas of such Enlightenment thinkers as Kant and Beccaria—ideas that antedated notions of rehabilitation that emerged in the nineteenth century" (von Hirsch, 1976:6).[4]

But Beccaria should also be acclaimed as a prophet among the current generation of conflict and radical scholars. Was it not Beccaria who first attacked the laws that were imposed by those above, to restrain those below? Said he: "[W]ho made these laws? The rich and the great, who never deigned to visit the miserable hut of the poor, who never see him dividing a piece of mouldy bread, amidst the cries of his famished children and the tears of his wife. Let us break those ties, fatal to the greatest part of mankind, and only useful to a few indolent tyrants'' (p. 103). In the introduction to his *Essay* Beccaria summed up his radicalism in these words: ''In every society there is an effort continually tending to confer on one part the height of power and happiness, and reduce the other to the extreme of weakness and misery'' (p. *xii*).

Such words could well have been written by any of the contemporary radical theorists who hold, as Quinney put it, that ''the state is organized to serve the interests of the dominant economic class, the capitalist ruling class,'' and that ''criminal law is an instrument the state and dominant ruling class use to maintain and perpetuate the social and economic order'' (1975:199). Yet Quinney, as we noted earlier, overlooks Beccaria's radical stance and regards him as simply another conservative supporter of the capitalist system (1979:n. 5).

The somewhat less radical conflict criminologists, likewise, should embrace Beccaria's motto. As Chambliss and Seidman put it, virtually in Beccarian terms: ''[S]ociety is composed of groups that are in conflict with one another. . . . [T]he law represents an institutionalized tool of those in power (ruling class) which functions to provide them with superior moral as well as coercive power in conflict'' (1971:504). Austin Turk further echoes Beccaria's conflict motto when he pronounces that ''criminality is not a biological, psychological, or even behavioral phenomenon, but a social status defined by the way in which an individual is perceived, evaluated, and treated by legal authorities'' (1969:25). According to this view, those who make the laws have the self-perpetuating power to make these laws, with which they are enabled to shape and manipulate all of society's institutions.

Some of Beccaria's contemporaries lamented that he had not said enough. The Abbé Gabriel de Mably demanded revolutionary social and political changes in order to remove the glaring inequalities which accounted for so much crime (Young, 1987:161, n. 16). But Beccaria stopped short of calling for a revolution. Recognizing that it was bad laws, like those nurturing inequality, which caused much of crime, he simply called for new, good laws—to be achieved by consensus, in accordance with the social contract theory of Montesquieu, Rousseau, Voltaire, and their brethren of the Enlightenment: ''[L]aws . . . are or ought to be conventions between men in a state of freedom." (p. *xii*). "Their only end in view, [is] the greatest happiness of the greatest number" (p. *xii*).

Beccaria also ought to be heralded by modern mainstream criminologists. What could Beccaria have had in mind when he postulated: "[Y]et another method of preventing crime is to reward virtue" (p. 156)? One of the principal propositions of Sutherland's theory of differential association comes to mind: "[A] person becomes delinquent because of an excess of definitions favorable to violation of law over definitions unfavorable to violation of law" (Sutherland and Cressey, 1978:81). Consequently, with his reward-based philosophy, Beccaria suggests that crime is, indeed, a learned behavior.

Moreover, did he not anticipate culture-conflict theorists to such an extent that they should acknowledge the heritage? Said Beccaria: "The credibility of a witness [or for that matter, any human being] may also be diminished by his being a member of a private [or, perhaps any *other*] society, whose custom and principles of conduct are either not known or are different from those of the public. Such a man has not only his own passions, but those of the society of which he is a member" (pp. 50–51). Compare this insight with the credo of culture-conflict theorists. As put by Thorsten Sellin: "There are social groups on the surface of the earth which possess complexes of conduct norms which, due to differences in the mode of life and the social values evolved by these groups, appear to set them apart from other groups in many or most respects. We may expect conflicts of norms. . . . [C]ulture conflicts are the natural outgrowth of processes of social differentiation, which produce an infinity of social groupings, each with its own definitions of life situations, its own interpretations of social relationships, its own ignorance or misunderstanding of the social values of other groups" (Sellin, 1938:63).

And may we add social-control theorists to the list of those foreshadowed by Beccaria, who observed "that by justice I understand nothing more than that *bond* which is necessary to keep the interest of individuals united, without which men would return to their original state of barbarity" (p. 19; emphasis added)! Is that at all different from Travis Hirschi's characterization of bonds within control theories: "Control theories assume that delinquent acts result when an individual's bond to society is weak or broken.

Since these theories embrace two highly complex concepts, the *bond* of an individual to *society,* it is not surprising that they have at one time or another formed the basis of explanations of most forms of aberrant or unusual behavior. It is also not surprising that control theories have described the elements of the bond to society in many ways, and that they have focused on a variety of units as the point of control" (Hirschi, 1969:16). Hirschi sums up control theory in general in these terms: "Control theory remains what it has always been: a theory in which deviation is not problematic. The question 'why do they do it?' is simply not the question the theory is designed to answer. The question is 'why don't we do it?' There is much evidence that we would if we dared" (1969:34). Let us hear Beccaria on control theory: "No man ever gave up his liberty merely for the good of the public. Such a chimera exists only in romances. Every individual wishes, if possible, to be exempt from the compacts that bind the rest of mankind" (p. 18). So much for amoral man in a society needing control.

Beccaria ought also to be acclaimed as a prophet by those who champion a scientific, research-oriented outlook. His program was not just an idealistic armchair contemplation of human nature, but one that referred to science as much as it was then possible to do. While this may be regarded by today's critics as prescientific, it was scientific in its time. In one of his passages—the crucial one on the establishment of an appropriate scale of punishments—he virtually envisaged modern research methodology. Said he: "If mathematical calculations could be applied to the obscure and infinite combination of human actions, there might be a corresponding scale of punishments, descending from the greatest to the least" (p. 30). Sellin and Wolfgang did precisely that in 1964. In their own words: "By means of scaling we have assigned numbers to certain components of events . . . and the analysis of the data has consisted in manipulating or operating on these numbers" (Sellin and Wolfgang, 1964:340–41). Thus, "the obscure and infinite combination of human actions" were ordered, elucidated, and measured in a manner that Beccaria envisaged but saw as impossible by the scientific equipment of his time.

Beccaria aimed at a scale of punishments to correspond to the gravity or weight of given criminal actions. He put his quest this way: "A scale of crimes may be formed, of which the first degree should consist of those which immediately tend to the dissolution of society, and the least of the smallest possible injustice done to a private member of that society. Between these extremes will be comprehended all actions contrary to the public good which are called criminal, and which descend by insensible degree, decreasing from the highest to the lowest'' (pp. 29–30). Two centuries later (1977), a *National Survey of Crime Severity* was designed and conducted by the Center for Studies in Criminology and Criminal Law (now called the Thorsten Sellin Center) at the University of Pennsylvania. It took ratings from sixty thousand respondents to develop a single severity score for each of 204 items. Highly sophisticated mathematical techniques were used to come up with scores that represent relationships of all crimes to each other in terms of seriousness (see U.S. Department of Justice, 1984).

Beccaria ought also to be recognized as the prophet of those modern crime-prevention specialists who posit that criminal justice alone cannot prevent criminality. He stood for the proposition that one must reform all parts of the entire social system in a purposeful manner in order to achieve crime reduction. Let us look at his views of society: there is, first of all, his view on the economic structure of society, to which I have already alluded, and its relationship to criminality. Second, there is his enlightened view on the role of education. Said he: ''[T]he most certain method of preventing crime is to perfect the system of education'' (p. 157). Third, as for politics, said he: ''Would you prevent crimes? Let liberty be attended with knowledge'' (p. 151). Fourth, on the role of the civil service, said he: ''Another method of preventing crime is, to make observance of the laws, and not their violation, the interest of the magistrate'' (p. 155). Fifth, on legislative policy, said he: ''Yet another method of preventing crime is to reward virtue'' (p. 156). Sixth, on the role of religion in society, he clearly recognized the relationship between God and human souls, and the role that the concepts of sin and punishment in the hereafter play. The criminal law, as created by human legislators, so it seemed to Beccaria, is merely a supplement to the higher law (p. 34). Seventh, Beccaria did not ignore the role of the family in the maintenance of a virtuous, that is, a crime-free, society (p. 90). All of these policy recognitions make it apparent that Beccaria had a holistic view of society, within which criminal justice is merely a component part.

Beccaria also ought to be acclaimed a prophet by those of us who, in recent decades, have begun to think of criminal justice as a system (and a subsystem of the overall social system), composed of interdependent component parts (or processes). Two hundred years before most of us went about in earnest in our efforts to make criminal-justice-system theory a reality, Beccaria had already recognized that, to make for effective and humane crime prevention, one has to reform and adjust all parts of what is indeed a system of criminal justice, within an overall social system. Clearly, to Beccaria, criminal justice is a coherent system that interrelates the making of laws and the breaking of laws. From penal legislation, with emphasis on the responsibility of legislators, to the prosecution of criminal cases, with emphasis on the role of the judge, the trustworthiness of evidence, and the participation of peers (jurors) in the judicial process, to the end product of *crime prevention,* Beccaria presented the blueprint for a criminal justice system. This novelty of 1764 is only now, gradually, becoming a reality.

Above all, Beccaria ought to be recognized as the prophet of all of us who seek to protect human rights inside and outside the criminal justice system: there is his staunch support for legality in criminal law (chaps. 3 and 5); his total rejection of torture in any form, whether to extract confessions or to punish culprits (chap. 16); his insistence on equality before the law (p. 80); his opposition to capital punishment (except in the clearest cases of national self-defense) (p. 98); and even his visionary view of gender equality in criminal justice (his demand that women be fully qualified as witnesses) (p. 48).

We have now gained a view of Beccaria that differs drastically from the one so frequently and superficially held nowadays—the view of Beccaria as merely the founder of the classical school (which supposedly could not reconcile retributism with utilitarianism). Rather, Beccaria emerges as the sum total of enlightened crime prevention and criminal justice, the advocate of a rational system of criminal justice within the body corporate of society as a whole.

There remains a disturbing thought. If Just Deserts theorists and utilitarians, for example, incapacitation advocates, cannot find common penological ground and regard their theories as irreconcilable, how can Beccaria's advocacy of both theories be reconciled?

If critical criminology and mainstream theory are at odds with each other in their search for the causes of crime, how can Beccaria not be at odds with himself when he, in effect, endorses both approaches—long before they had matured into theory? The problem is, of course, ours, and not Beccaria's. He wrote against an incredibly cruel and unenlightened way of dealing with the crime problem. His thoughts were enlightened then and still are today. Marc Ancel called Beccaria the "apostle of legality but enemy of formalism and technical legalism" (Ancel, 1987:135). It is indeed humanism which is the hallmark of Beccaria's work. Beccaria "crystallized, defined, and gave form to the still confused aspiration of his age" (Ancel, 1987:22). Perhaps our aspirations are still confused—and seemingly irreconcilable. The only common bond in all the seemingly conflicting desiderata of Beccaria's *Essay,* as in the schools of thought that owe their property to Beccaria, is humanism. Beccaria did not try to reconcile what to us are conflicting points of view; he was not sufficiently equipped as a philosopher to do so, nor was the need for reconciliation apparent at that time. For us to engage in an effort to reconcile Beccaria's thoughts would seem to be an exercise in futility. We are prone to identify Beccaria, ex post facto, with the Classical School, which seems unwarranted in view of the fact that he championed virtually every other (humanistic) school. But that should not be our principal concern. Our concern should be that of the *practical* impact of his humanism on world development.

Let me, then, finally pose the question: How far have we succeeded in implementing Cesare Beccaria's humanistic program? Let us look at the record as a whole, as represented in the United Nations—well noting that some nations are ahead, while others are still struggling to catch up with various points of Beccaria's program.

- Beccaria's resolute rejection of *torture* was documented through the *Declaration on the Protection of All Persons from Being Subjected to Torture and Other Cruel, Inhuman, or Degrading Treatment or Punishment* by the Fifth United Nations Congress on the Prevention of Crime and the Treatment of Offenders, at Geneva, 1975—but not until then! (U.N. General Assembly, 1975). Today the ban on torture is contained both in the *Code of*

Conduct for Law Enforcement Officials (U.N. General Assembly, 1979), and in the *Convention against Torture and Other Cruel, Inhuman or Degrading Treatment or Punishment* (U.N. General Assembly, 1984).

- That same convention embodies Beccaria's ban on *cruel and unnecessary infliction of pain for the sake of punishment*.
- As for Beccaria's virtual rejection of *capital punishment*, the United Nations has adopted *the Safeguards Guaranteeing Protection of the Rights of Those Facing the Death Penalty* (U.N. Economic and Social Council (ECOSOC), 1984), and expressed its deep alarm at the occurrence on a large scale of summary and arbitrary executions (U.N. General Assembly, 1983), all within the stated purpose of the eventual abolition of capital punishment (U.N. ECOSOC, 1971).
- Beccaria's demand for the humane treatment of imprisoned persons (Beccaria, 1819:169) has been met by the *United Nations Standard Minimum Rules for the Treatment of Prisoners* (U.N. ECOSOC, 1957).
- His views on the political independence of the judiciary, and their dependence on the law, was incorporated in the *United Nations Basic Principles of the Judiciary* (U.N. General Assembly, 1985b).
- His demand for education of the public in the premises of law, long practiced in the socialist countries, was met by the Sixth United Nations Congress on the Prevention of Crime and the Treatment of Offenders, in Caracas, 1980 (U.N. Resolution, 1981), and is now the subject of the very first joint empirical research by American and Soviet criminologists.[5]
- Beccaria even envisaged the possibility—some time in the future—of returning prisoners to their home countries for the service of a penal sentence imposed abroad (p. 136). That policy is being promoted by the United Nations through the *Model Agreement on the Transfer of Foreign Prisoners and Recommendations on the Treatment of Foreign Prisoners* (U.N. General Assembly, 1985a).
- Beccaria's demand for open and public trials is enshrined today in the *International Covenant on Civil and Political Rights* (U.N. General Assembly, 1966).

In conclusion, I invite you to make this cultural experiment. Look at the prints or panoramic etchings of any of the great cities of Europe. Compare those produced before Cesare Beccaria's time with those produced later. You will find an amazing difference. The older prints feature prominently the city gallows. In the post-Beccaria prints the gallows are conspicuous through their absence. Thus, it appears that Beccaria may, indeed, have been responsible for changing our outlook on crime, on life, and on death. Before Beccaria, crime, like poverty and death, seemed inevitable, and thus the gallows on the panoramic city prints. After Beccaria, there was hope that societies could *manage* their affairs, and could control crime, punishment, life, and death.

Notes

1. Cesare Beccaria-Bonesana. *An Essay on Crimes and Punishments* (with commentary by M. D. Voltaire). 2nd American ed. Philadelphia: Philip H. Nicklin. 1819. All references hereinafter refer to this edition. The first American edition was published in New York in 1773.
2. That Wilson no longer endorses the original policy with equal fervor is here of no consequence. See the National Academy of Sciences report of a committee chaired by Alfred Blumstein, and cosigned by James Q. Wilson, *Deterrence and Incapacitation: Estimating the Effects of Criminal Sanctions on Crime Rates,* edited by Alfred Blumstein, Jacqueline Cohen, and Daniel Nagin, pp. 3–90.
3. Andrew von Hirsch, however, rejects Beccaria's proportionality principle as being utilitarian and therefore having lost its character as "an independent ethical requirement" (1985:32).
4. For subsequent acknowledgements see von Hirsch (1985:31–32) where, however, he stresses Beccaria's emphasis on deterrence within an overall framework of retribution.
5. The research in progress is being conducted jointly by Dr. James O. Finckenauer, Rutgers University; Dr. June Tapp, University of Minnesota; Dr. Alexander M. Jacovlev, Institute of State and Law, U.S.S.R. Academy of Sciences.

References

Ancel, Marc. 1987. *Social Defense* (publication of the Comparative Criminal Law Project, vol. 16). Littleton, Colo.: Fred B. Rothman and Co.

Beccaria, Cesare Bonesana. [1764] 1819. *An Essay on Crimes and Punishments* (with commentary by M. D. Voltaire). 2nd American ed. Philadelphia: Philip H. Nicklin.

Bentham, Jeremy. [1789] 1892. *Introduction to the Principles of Morals and Legislation*. Oxford: Clarendon Press.

Binder, Arnold, Gilbert Geis, and Dickson Bruce. 1988. *Juvenile Delinquency: Historical, Cultural, Legal Perspectives*. New York: MacMillan Publishing Co.

Chambliss, William, and Robert Seidman. 1971. *Law, Order, and Power*. Reading: Addison-Wesley.

Greenwood, Peter. 1982. *Selective Incapacitation*. Santa Monica: Rand Corp.

Hagan, John. 1985. *Modern Criminology: Crime, Criminal Behavior, and Its Control*. New York: McGraw-Hill Book Co.

Haskell, Martin R., and Lewis Yablonski. 1983. *Criminology: Crime and Criminality*. 3rd ed. Boston: Houghton Mifflin Co.

Hirshi, Travis. 1969. *Causes of Delinquency*. Berkeley: University of California Press.

Lipton, Douglas, Robert Martinson, and Judith Wilks. 1975. *The Effectiveness of Correctional Treatment: A Survey of Treatment Evaluation Studies*. New York: Praeger.

Mannle, Henry W., and J. David Hirschel. 1982. *Fundamentals of Criminology*. Albany, N.Y.: Delmar Publisher, Inc.

Martinson, Robert. 1974. "What Works?—Questions and Answers about Prison Reform." *Journal of Public Interest* 6:22–54.

Monachesi, Elio. 1960. "Cesare Beccaria." In *Pioneers in Criminology*, edited by Hermann Mannheim, pp. 36–50. Chicago: Quadrangle Books.

Moore, Mark, Susan Estrich, Daniel McGillis, and William Spelman. 1985. *Dangerous Offenders: The Elusive Target of Justice*. Cambridge, Mass.: Harvard University Press.

Morgan, Edmund S. 1965. *Puritan Political Ideas*. Indianapolis: Bobbs-Merrill Co.

Quinney, Richard. 1975. "Crime Control in Capitalist Society." In *Critical Criminology*, edited by Jan Taylor, Paul Walton, and Jack Young. London: Routledge and Kegan Paul.

———. 1979. *Criminology*. 2nd ed. Boston: Little, Brown, and Company.

Reid, Sue Titus. 1985. *Crime and Criminology*. 4th ed. New York: Holt, Rinehart, and Winston.

———. 1987. *Criminal Justice: Procedures and Issues*. St. Paul: West Publishing Co.

Rogers, Joseph W., and G. Larry Mays. 1987. *Juvenile Delinquency and Juvenile Justice*. New York: John Wiley and Sons.

Sellin, Thorsten. 1980. *The Penalty of Death*. Beverly Hills: Sage Publications.

———. 1938. *Culture Conflict and Crime*. Bulletin no. 41. New York: Social Science Research Council.

Sellin, Thorsten, and Marvin E. Wolfgang. 1964. *The Measurement of Delinquency*. New York: John Wiley and Sons.

Siegel, Larry J. 1983. *Criminology*. St. Paul: West Publishing Co.

Sutherland, Edwin H., and Donald R. Cressey. 1978. *Criminology*. 10th ed. Philadelphia: J. B. Lippincott Co.

Turk, Austin. 1969. *Criminality and Legal Order*. Chicago: Rand McNally.

U.N. Economic and Social Council (ECOSOC). 1957. Res. 663 C I (XXIV) of 31 July, as amended by ECOSOC Res. 2076 (LXII) of 13 May 1977.

————. 1984. Res. 1984/50. 25 May.

————. 1971. Res. 1574 (L).

U.N. General Assembly. 1966. Res. 2200 A (XXI), Art. 14. 16 Dec.

————. 1975. Res. 3452 (XXX). 9 Dec.

————. 1979. Res. 34/169. 17 Dec.

————. 1983. Res. 38/96. 16 Dec.

————. 1984. Res. 39/46. 10 Dec.

————. 1985a. Res. 40/32. 29 Nov.

————. 1985b. Res. 40/146. 13 Dec.

————. Res. 2857 (XXVI).

U.N. Resolution. 1981. Resolution 15. A/CONF. 87/14/Rev. 1.

U.S. Department of Justice. 1984. "The Security of Crime." Bureau of Justice Statistics Bulletin. Jan.

von Hirsch, Andrew. 1976. *Doing Justice—The Choice of Punishment*. New York: Hill and Woung.

————. 1985. *Past or Future Crimes*. New Brunswick, N.J.: Rutgers University Press.

Wilson, James Q. 1975. *Thinking about Crime*. New York: Basic Books.

Wolfgang, Marvin E. 1979. "Current Trends in Penal Philosophy." *Israeli Law Review* 14:427.

Young, David B. 1983. "Cesare Beccaria: Utilitarian or Retributivist?" *Journal of Criminal Justice* 11:317–26.

————. 1987. " 'Let Us Content Ourselves with Praising the Work While Drawing a Veil over Its Principles': Eighteenth Century Reactions to Beccaria's *On Crime and Punishments*." *Justice Quarterly* 1(2):156–69.

2

On the Plausibility of
Corporate Crime Theory

John Braithwaite and Brent Fisse

The Australian National University was graced with a lively series of seminars in 1986 in which Donald Cressey presented his latest thoughts on white-collar crime. The first volume of *Advances in Criminological Theory* published the most striking contribution from those presentations, "The Poverty of Theory in Corporate Crime Research." One of us suggested to Cressey in 1986 that we might submit a critique of his paper to *Advances in Criminological Theory,* in the hope that we might replicate the stimulating exchange at those Canberra seminars. His tragic death intervened and we abandoned the idea. Now we suspect this was the wrong decision.

There is a sense in which "The Poverty of Theory in Corporate Crime Research" is a critique of the younger Cressey by the older Cressey. In characteristic style, Cressey catalogued the failings in his earlier work on juvenile gangs, La Cosa Nostra "families," prisons, and corporations. The failing he attributed to his younger self was that of treating organizations as if they were unitary persons.

Donald Cressey was a great criminologist. He had his influence because he was majestically contentious, unreservedly iconoclastic. No one revered Edwin Sutherland more than Donald Cressey; yet in "The Poverty of Theory in Corporate Crime Research,"

Cressey accuses Sutherland of being "unthinking," "assaulting his own common sense" by anthropomorphizing corporations. Some insight into this irreverence is revealed in John Laub's oral history, where it is reported that Cressey perceived his influence on criminology as "mostly in getting people going on things. I like to go in and get something started and stirred up. Then I leave it and let other people worry about the details" (Laub, 1983:16).

Cressey was at his provocative best in his last article, in which he delighted in the mischief of attacking both the younger Cressey and the older Sutherland for failing to be true to the promise of the younger Sutherland. But if we are to reap the true harvest of Cressey's intellect, we do not have to take one side or the other; rather, we must perceive the dialectic between the younger and the older Cressey.

In playing our part to enliven this dialectic, we cannot but be struck by the ironies of Cressey's intellectual history. Sutherland's theory was in important ways a reaction against the psychological ascendancy in criminology during his lifetime. Cressey's great theoretical contribution was to build on differential association in a way that transcended the empty theoretical divisions between psychology and sociology. His masterly presidential address to the Pacific Sociological Association thirty years ago staked out the challenge for criminological theory (Cressey, 1960). This was to develop a theory that explained not only why some individuals engaged in more crime or different kinds of crime from other individuals, but also why some structural contexts show higher crime rates and different crime patterns than others. Cressey was decades ahead of his time in formulating criminology's agenda for integrating micro and macro levels of analysis. He was frustrated in his lifetime by the failure of his criminological peers to pursue integrated micro-macro explanations, and particularly frustrated by the crude methodological holism of most of his sociological contemporaries. This frustration, we suspect, led Cressey to adopt more extremist methodological individualist positions in order to jolt and provoke us. Only Don Cressey could give a speech entitled "Everybody's Wrong" (Colomy, 1988:256). So let us be provoked in the hope that we will ultimately find the individualist-holist synthesis for which Cressey himself yearned.

The thrust of "The Poverty of Theory in Corporate Crime

Research'' is to call into question seven assumptions that are common in corporate crime research:

1. Corporations are like real persons.
2. Corporations act.
3. Corporations have intentions.
4. Corporations have legal and ethical responsibilities.
5. Corporations can commit crime.
6. Corporations can suffer from punishment.
7. The same theory can be applied to individual and corporate criminals.

It is also important to understand what Cressey did not want to say. As a matter of public policy he did not want to abandon the "legal fiction" that corporations are persons because "this legal fiction is essential to fairness" (Cressey, 1988:34). If corporations were not assigned the legal characteristics of persons, no one could sue them or make contracts with them. He also rather equivocally concedes the practical necessity of holding corporations criminally liable for wrongdoing perpetrated by their executives, given that these executives are "masters at using the corporate form to mask their misbehavior" (1988:36). Our contention will be that corporate criminal responsibility is defensible as more than just an expedient legal fiction. Second, we will defend the position that sound scientific theories can be based on a foundation of corporate action, and that some theories of individual action can also usefully be applied to corporate action.

Corporations Are Like Real Persons

Cressey's contention here is that "anyone who tries to understand white-collar crime is severely handicapped by the fiction that corporations are disembodied political, social and economic persons who behave just like ordinary men and women" (1988:34). Cressey correctly points out that first, corporations can do many things individuals cannot: "They can buy and sell each other legally, as though the 'person' being sold were a slave" (1988:34). Because the makeup of a corporation is different from that of a human being, it can do things that are not humanly possible, such as growing from infant to adult in a year, securing immortality. Second, in other ways the corporation is less than a person: it cannot feel human emotions.

This much is unexceptionable. Many of us have been guilty of slipping into a forgetfulness of the fundamental differences between corporations and human beings under the seductive influence of the simplifying language of corporate personhood. But this does not mean that there are no ways in which corporations and human beings are similar. What matters is whether there are some theoretically relevant similarities. For some purposes, we can usefully model individual human conduct as rational goal-seeking behavior. For some purposes, we can usefully model corporate conduct as rational goal-seeking behavior.

Some philosophical debates about what the theoretically relevant differences and similarities are between individuals and corporations have been difficult and perplexing. Peter French (1984, 1986) contends that corporations are moral persons because they manifest intentionality, while many other philosophers contend that much more than a capacity to act intentionally is required for moral personhood (Dan-Cohen, 1986; De George, 1986; Ladd, 1986; Donaldson, 1982, 1986; May, 1986). Corporations clearly have a different metaphysical status from individuals; being formed for limited purposes, they do not have the same status as ends in themselves as do human beings (De George, 1986:60). Corporations are not moral persons in the sense of enjoying all of the rights that human beings properly enjoy, such as a right to life (Ladd, 1986). But we do not have to regard corporations as moral persons to hold them responsible for their actions.

The important question for criminological theory is not whether corporations are moral persons but whether corporations are capable of criminal action and whether they can properly be held responsible. A theory of criminal responsibility need not and should not depend on the metaphysical status of moral personhood. Our task is to develop a theory of what it means to be criminally responsible, and then to ask whether corporations are capable of the kind of action that that entails. But first we must ask whether corporations can act at all, something that Cressey called into question.

Corporations Act

In adopting the view that corporations do not act, that only individuals act, Cressey not only questions the idea of corporate crime but casts doubt on the whole enterprise of organizational sociology. Cressey shares the methodological individualism that Hayek formulated as follows: "There is no other way toward an understanding of social phenomena but through our understanding of individual actions directed toward other people and guided by their expected behavior" (1949:6).

Methodological individualism as advocated by Hayek (1949) and Popper (1947) amounts to an ontology that only individuals are real in the social world, while social phenomena like corporations are abstractions that cannot be directly observed. This ontology is spurious (Lukes, 1973). The notion that individuals are real, observable, flesh and blood, while corporations are legal fictions is false. Plainly, many features of corporations are observable (their assets, factories, decision-making procedures), while many features of individuals are not (for example, personality, intention, unconscious mind) (cf. McDonald, 1987). Both individuals and corporations are defined by a mix of observable and abstracted characteristics.

Clifford Geertz contends that "the Western conception of the person as a bounded, unique, more or less integrated emotional and cognitive universe, a dynamic centre of awareness, emotion, judgment, and action organized into a distinctive whole . . . is a rather peculiar idea within the context of the world's cultures" (1983:59). Reflecting upon his anthropological fieldwork, Geertz cites Balinese culture, wherein it is dramatis personae, not actors, that endure or indeed exist:

> Physically men come and go, mere incidents in a happenstance history, of no genuine importance even to themselves. But the masks they wear, the stage they occupy, the parts they play, and, most important, the spectacle they mount remain, and comprise not the façade but the substance of things, not least the self. Shakespeare's old-trouper view of the vanity of action in the face of mortality—all the world's a stage and we are but poor players, content to strut our hour, and so on—

makes no sense here. There is no make-believe; of course players perish, but the play does not, and it is the latter, the performed rather than the performer that really matters [Geertz, 1983:62].

The merging of the individual person with the land in Australian aboriginal cultures, where a particular rock can be part of an ancestor or part of oneself, provides another example at odds with the conception of bounded unitary individualism. Even within the Western cultural tradition it is difficult to accept that individuals, unlike corporations, are characterized by a bounded unitary consciousness. As Hindess (1988) has pointed out, decisions made by individuals as well as those made by corporations have a diffuse grounding; they represent the product of "diverse and sometimes conflicting objectives, forms of calculation, and means of action." When the sober John Smith expresses remorse at the way John Smith behaves when he is drunk, this disassociation of self illustrates that the individual is not such a unitary self (Goffman, 1971:113). When scholars speak of defending some of the alleged sins of the younger Cressey against the older Cressey, they can fracture the unitary conception of this individual without questioning that Cressey was capable of action.

The polar opposite to methodological individualism is the methodological holism of the early European sociologists, notably Emile Durkheim. For Durkheim, "the individual finds himself in the presence of a force [society] which is superior to him and before which he bows" (1966:123). From this perspective, the collective will of society is not the product of the individual consciousness of members of society (Durkheim, 1911). Quite the reverse: the individual is the product of social forces.

Both the crude methodological individualism of Hayek and the crude methodological holism of Durkheim are unpersuasive. It is just as constricting to see the sailor as the navy writ small as it is to see the navy as the sailor writ large. It is true to say that the activity of the navy is constituted by the actions of individual sailors. But it is also true that the existence of a sailor is constituted by the existence of the navy. Take away the institutional framework of the navy—ships, captains, rules of war, other sailors—and the notion of an individual sailor makes no sense. Institutions are constituted by individuals, and individuals are socially constituted by institutions (Giddens, 1979, 1984). To conceive of corporations as no more than sums of the isolated efforts of individuals would be as foolish as to conceive the possibility of language without the interactive processes of individuals talking to one another and passing structures of syntax from one generation to another.

Irving Thalberg and others have suggested that "it would be absurd to say that corporations could act even though all human beings have perished" (May, 1983:79–80). In fact it is not absurd. If all humankind perished in a nuclear war and preprogrammed missiles of the U.S. Army continued to be launched, why could we not describe their launching as an action of the U.S. Army (see also Dan-Cohen, 1986; Held, 1986)? Thompson points out that part of the genius of modern organizations is their capacity to perform tasks of spectacular complexity when set against the rather ordinary individual talents of the people involved. This genius can be understood in terms of the composition of these individual talents into a corporate system. To look for the answer as a simple sum of individual genius is to commit a "fallacy of division" (Thompson, 1986:117).

Equally misguided is a sociological determinism that grants no intentionality to individuals, that sees them as wholly shaped by macrosociological forces. Sociological functionalism, as championed by Durkheim, indulges this absurdity. Mesmerized by the achievements of evolutionary theory in biology, the functionalists failed to recognize that human beings are capable of reflecting upon causal laws and engaging in purposive social action that does not conform to those laws or, indeed, that is intended to defeat them. We may readily agree with Durkheim that each kind of community is a thought world that penetrates and moulds the minds of its members, but that is not to deny the capacity of individuals to exercise their autonomy to resist and reshape thought worlds.

All wholes are made up of parts; reductionism can be a near-infinite regress. Psychological reductionists can argue that the behavior of organizations can only be understood by analyzing the behavior of individual members of the organization. Biological reductionists can argue that the behavior of individuals can only be understood by the behavior of parts of the body—firing synapses in the brain, hormonal changes, movement of a hand across a page. Chemical reductionists might argue that these body parts can only be understood as movements of molecules. At all of these levels of analysis, reductionism is blinkered because the whole is always more than the sum of the individual parts; in each case there is a need to build upon reductionism to study how the parts interact to form wholes. In the case of organizations, individuals may be the most important parts, but there are other parts, as is evident from factories with manifest routines that operate to some extent independently of the biological agents who flick the switches. Organizations are "socio-technical" systems (Emery, 1969), not just aggregations of individuals. More crucially, however, organizations consist of sets of expectations about how different kinds of problems should be resolved. These expectations are a sediment of the individual expectations of many past and present members of the organization. But they are also a product of the *interplay* among individuals' views. The interaction between individual and shared expectations, on the one hand, and the organization's environment, on the other, continually reproduces shared expectations. In other words, an organization has a culture which is transmitted from one generation of organizational role incumbents to the next. Indeed, the entire personnel of an organization may change without reshaping the corporate culture; this may be so even if the new incumbents have personalities quite different from those of the old.

The products of organizations are more than the sum of the products of individual actions; while each member of the board of directors can "vote" for a declaration of dividend, only the board as a collectivity is empowered to declare a dividend. The collective action is thus qualitatively different from the human actions that, in part, constitute it. "Groupthink" (Janis, 1972) and the group risky-shift phenomenon (Wallach, Kogan, and Bem, 1964) also illustrate how collective expectations can be quite different from the sum of individual expectations. A number of psychological studies suggest that group decision making can make members of the group willing to accept stupid ideas or hazardous risks that they would reject if making the same decision alone (but see Janis and Mann, 1977:423).

Cressey underpins his questioning of the concept of corporate criminal liability by suggesting that organizations do not think, decide, or act; these are all things done by individuals. So we are told that it is a crass anthropomorphism to say that the White House decided upon a course of action, or that the United States declared war. Instead we should say that the president decided and that the president and a majority of members of Congress decided to go to war. If saying that "the White House decided" connotes that "the White House" would decide in the same way as an individual person, then we are certainly engaging in anthropomorphism. Yet people who decode such messages understand that organizations emit decisions just as individuals do, but that they reach these decisions in a rather different way. They fully accept that "the White House decided" is a simplification given that many actors typically have a say in such decisions. Nevertheless, it is probably less of a simplification than the statement "the president decided." Indeed, it may be fanciful to individualize a collective product. The president may never have turned his mind to the decision: he may have done no more than waive his power to veto it, or he may have delegated the decision totally.

Similarly, it makes more sense to say that the United States has declared war than to say that the president and a majority of Congress have decided to do so. A declaration of war commits many more individuals and physical resources to purposive social action than the individuals who voted for it; it commits the United States as a whole to war, and many individuals outside the Congress participate or acquiesce in making the commitment:

> A man does not have to agree with his government's acts to see himself embodied in them any more than he has to approve of his own acts to acknowledge that he has, alas, performed them. It is a question of immediacy, of experiencing what the state "does" as proceeding naturally from a familiar and intelligible "we" [Geertz, 1973:317].

The temptation to reduce such decisions to the actions of individuals is widespread, as in the suggestion, once common, that wars be settled by a fistfight or duel between the protagonist heads of state.

The expression "the White House decided" is a social construction; as a matter of social construction, the same organizational output might be expressed as "the president decided" or "the administration decided" or "the United States decided" or "the president gave in to the decision of the Congress." Equally, the concept of "deciding" is a social construct (what amounts to "deciding" for some is "muddling through" or perhaps even "ducking a decision" for others). To talk of individual decisions as real and of collective decisions as fictions, as Cressey does, is to obscure the inevitability of social construction at any level of analysis.

In many circumstances the social construction "the White House decided" will be a workable one for analytic purposes. This does not mean that we should treat this as the only accurate description of what happened any more than we should accept "the president decided" as the real description of what happened. Indeed, the social control of corporate crime depends on understanding how those involved with a crime socially construct the responsible individuals or collectivity. The key to unlocking the control of corporate crime is granting credibility to multiple social construc-tions of responsbility, and investigating the processes of generating and invoking these social constructions; as Geertz has explained, "[h]opping back and forth between the whole conceived through the parts that actualize it and the parts conceived through the whole that motivates them, we seek to turn them, by a sort of intellectual perpetual motion, into explications of one another" (1973:317).

Social theory and legal theory are thus forced to stake out positions between individualism and holism. The task is to explore how wholes are created out of purposive individual action, and how individual action is constituted and constrained by the structural realities of wholes. This exploration extends to how responsibility for action in the context of collectivities is socially constructed by those involved as well as by outsiders. Moral responsibility can be meaningfully allocated when conventions for allocating responsibil-ity are shared by insiders and understood by outsiders. Metaphys-ics about the distinctive, unitary, irreducible agency of individuals tend to obstruct analysis, as do metaphysics about the special features of corporateness. As elaborated in the following section, the moral responsibility of corporations for their actions relates essentially to social processes and not to elusive attributes of personhood; as Surber has indicated, the issue is "more a matter of what we consider moral responsibility to be, rather than what sort of metaphysical entities corporations may turn out to be" (1983:81).

Corporations Have Intentions

Cressey contends that, because corporations are not real persons, they cannot have intentions; intention is something unique to being a person. While it is obviously true that corporations lack the capacity to entertain a cerebral mental state of intentionality, corporations manifest their own special kind of intentionality—corporate policy. Peter French identifies the Corporate Internal Decision Structure of corporations as a license of the sort required to redescribe certain corporate actions as intentional. To be intentional, just one of any number of true redescriptions of the behavior need involve intentionality. Hence, the depositing of money in a bank can be redescribed in a variety of purely mechanical ways, as well as in at least one intentional form. A Corporate Internal Decision Structure involves (1) an organizational system of stations and levels of decision-making, and (2) a set of decision/action recognition rules of two types: procedural and policy. "These recognition rules provide the tests that a decision or action was made for corporate reasons within the corporate decision structure" (French, 1986:22). French applies a Wittgensteinian (1975:39) distinction: the organizational structure supplies a grammar of the corporation's decision making, and the recognition rules provide its logic.

The concepts of corporate policies and procedures do not express merely the intentionality of a company's directors, officers, or employees, but they project the idea of a distinctly corporate strategy:

> It will be objected that a corporation's policies reflect only the current goals of its directors. But that is certainly not logically necessary nor is it in practice true for most large corporations. Usually, of course, the original incorporators will have organized to further their individual interests and/or to meet goals which they shared. [But] even in infancy the melding of disparate interests and purposes gives rise to a corporate long range point of view that is distinct from the intents and purposes of the collection of incorporators viewed individually [French, 1984:45–46].

While we accept French's account of a special corporate kind of intentionality that courts can sensibly recognize, one does not have to accept it to be able to hold corporations blameworthy or responsible for their actions. We will turn to this in the next section. But first we must dispense with Cressey's claim that unless behavior is intended, it cannot be explained:

> [I]t is just as ridiculous for criminologists to try to explain criminal behavior that was not intended as it is for judges to try to determine whether a fictitious person has an evil state of mind [1988:48].

> Because corporations cannot intend actions, none of their criminality can be explained in the framework of behavioral theory [1988:48].

> [N]o social psychological theory can make sense of behavior that is not intended, be it ordinary crime such as felony murder or a white-collar crime such as restraint of trade, false advertising, or unfair labor practices [1988:46].

Yet we know that psychological theories can and do explain behaviors that, instead of being intentional, are negligent or unconscious or a reflex. And if we move from micro to macro levels of explanation, intent as an essential ingredient of social explanation becomes even more suspect. An explanation of the Great Depression is not likely to be found by searching for people who intended it. So we must dismiss out of hand the suggestion that because corporate behavior cannot be intentional, it cannot be explained.

Corporations Have Legal and Ethical Responsibilities

Cressey considers talk of corporate citizenship, of corporate social responsibility, of a social contract imposing ethical and legal obligations on corporations as anthropomorphism. Good consequences might flow from people being deluded into accepting such fictions, but they are still anthropomorphisms. However, it is not clear why we can only talk of individuals as having responsibilities. Thus, De George, who does not believe that corporations are moral persons, can still argue that corporations are nevertheless subject to moral rules and are to blame for breaking them:

It suffices to recognize that as human creations which are used by human beings for certain ends and which can be said to act, corporations have the status of moral actors. A moral actor is subject to the moral law and one can correctly evaluate such an actor's actions from a moral point of view [De George, 1986:63].

What, then, is a sensible formulation of corporate moral responsibility or blameworthiness? Blameworthiness requires essentially two conditions: first, the ability of the actor to make decisions; second, the inexcusable failure of the actor to perform an assigned task. Herbert Simon (1965) has defined a formal organization as a "decision-making structure." Under this definition, a formal organization has one of the requirements for blameworthiness that a mob, for example, does not have. We routinely hold organizations responsible for a decision when and because that decision instantiates an organizational policy and instantiates an organizational decision-making process that the organization has chosen for itself. A decision made by a rogue individual in defiance of corporate policy (including unwritten corporate policy) to undermine corporate goals, or in flagrant disregard of corporate decision-making rules, is not a decision for which the organization is morally responsible. This is not to say, however, that we cannot hold the organization responsible if the intention of individuals is other than to promote corporate goals and policies. It may be that two individuals, A and B, hold the key to a particular corporate decision. A decides what to support because of a bribe; her intention is to collect the bribe rather than to advance corporate goals. B decides to support the same course of action out of a sense of loyalty to A, who is an important ally and mentor; his intention is formed from a consideration of bureaucratic politics rather than corporate goals. Even though the key individuals do not personally intend to further corporate policy by the decision, it may be that they cannot secure the acquiescence of the rest of the organization with the decision unless they can advance credible reasons as to why the decision will advance corporate policy. If the reasons given are accepted and acted on within the corporate decision-making process, then we can hold the corporation responsible irrespective of any games played by individual actors among themselves. It is not just that corporate intention (the instantiation of corporate policy in a decision) is more than the sum of individual intentions; it may have little to do with individual intentions.

Blameworthiness also requires an inexcusable failure to perform an assigned task (Goodin, 1987). Any culture confers certain types of responsibilities on certain kinds of actors. Fathers have responsibilities not to neglect their children. Doctors bear special responsibilities in the giving of medical advice. Just as fathers and doctors can be held to different and higher standards of responsibility by virtue of role or capacity, so it is possible for corporations to be held to different and higher standards of responsibility than individuals because of their role or capacity as organizations (Goodin, 1987).

It is not a legal fiction for the law to hold corporations responsible for their decisions; in all cultures it is common for citizens to do so. When the law adopts these cultural notions of corporate responsibility, it does more than reflect the culture: it deepens and shapes the notions of corporate responsibility already present in the culture. The law can clarify the content of what we expect corporations to be responsible for. Thus, the law can require large chemical companies to be responsible for an inventory of all hazardous chemicals on their premises, a responsibility not imposed on individual householders. More fundamentally, the law is not only presented with the cultural fact that a corporation can be blamed; the law, more than any other institution in the culture, is constantly implicated in reproducing that cultural fact. Thus, the Roman law tradition of treating corporate persons as fictions and the Germanic realist theory that law cannot create its subjects (that is, that corporations are preexisting sociological persons) both overlook the recursive nature of the relationship between law and culture (French, 1984:35–37). Corporations are held responsible for the outcomes of their policies and decision-making procedures partly because organizations have the capacity to change their policies and procedures. Thomas Donaldson (1982:22) has pointed out that, like corporations, a computer conducting a search and a cat waiting to pounce on a mouse are making decisions and are even doing so intentionally. We grant moral agency to the corporation and yet not to the cat or the computer for two reasons, according to Donaldson. First, the corporation, like the individual human being and unlike the cat, can give moral reasons for its decision making. Second, the corporation has the capacity to change its goals and policies and to change the decision-making processes directed at those goals and policies. For these reasons the concept of corporate intentionality defies equation with feline or digital brain waves.

Corporate intentionality does not exhaust the range of relevant fault concepts. We can blame actors for things done deliberately, where the actor does not want or intend harm, but is quite deliberate about being willing to run the risk of harm. In practice, the predominant form of corporate fault is more likely to be corporate negligence than corporate intention. Companies usually are at pains not to display any posture of inattention to legal requirements; on the contrary, compliance policies are de rigueur in companies that have given any thought to legal-risk minimization (Bruns, 1985; Sciamanda, 1987). Corporate negligence is prevalent where communication breakdowns occur, or where organizations suffer from collective oversight. Does corporate negligence in such a context amount merely to negligence on the part of individuals? It may be possible to explain the *causes* of corporate wrongdoing in terms of particular contributions by managers and employees, but the attribution of *fault* is another matter (Shaver, 1985). Corporate negligence does not necessarily reduce to individual negligence. A corporation may have a greater capacity for avoiding the commission of an offense, and for this reason it may be that a finding of corporate but not individual negligence may be justified. We may be reluctant to pass judgement on the top executives of Union Carbide for the Bhopal disaster (perhaps because of failures of communication within the organization about safety problems abroad), but higher standards of care are expected of such a company given its collective might and resources (Walter and Richards, 1986). Thus, where a corporate system is blamed for criminogenic group pressures, that blame is directed not at individual actors but, rather, at an institutional setup from which the expected standards of organizational performance are higher than the standards expected of any personnel (Cooper, 1972). As Donaldson has observed in the context of corporate intelligence:

Corporations can and should have access to practical and theoretical knowledge which dwarfs that of individuals. When Westinghouse Inc.

manufactures machinery for use in nuclear power generating plants, it should use its massive resources to consider tens of thousands of possible consequences and be able to weigh their likelihood accurately. Which human errors might occur? How are they to be handled? How might espionage occur? How should human systems interface with mechanized ones? . . . Good intentions for Westinghouse are not adequate. Westinghouse must have, in addition to good intentions, superhuman intelligence [1982:125].

Corporations, it may thus be argued, can be blamed and held morally responsible for intentional or negligent conduct. Michael McDonald has gone further by arguing that organizations are paradigm moral agents:

Not only does the organization have all the capacities that are standardly taken to ground autonomy—vis., capacities for intelligent agency—but it also has them to a degree no human can. Thus, for example, a large corporation has available and can make use of far more information than one individual can. Moreover, the corporation is in principle "immortal" and so better able to bear responsibility for its deeds than humans, whose sin dies with them [1987:219–20].

Granted, corporations lack human feelings and emotions, but this hardly disqualifies them from possessing the quality of autonomy. On the contrary, the lack of emotions and feelings promotes rather than hinders rational choice, and in this respect the corporation may indeed be a paradigm responsible actor (McDonald, 1987).

There are other difficulties with the view that corporate responsibility amounts to merely an aggregation of individual responsibility. Repeatedly in organizational life, individual actors contribute to collective decision-making processes without being conscious of the totality of that process—each individual actor is a part of a whole, which no one of them fully comprehends. Indeed, even that part that an individual contributes may be unconscious.

Consider the predicament of the campaigner for clearer writing who is concerned about the way children learn an excessive use of the passive voice when they should use the active voice. Our activist wants to allocate blame for the way children leave school with ingrained habits of overusing the passive voice. Empirically, he may find that in general neither students nor teachers have a conscious understanding of what it means to use the passive versus the active voice. Unconsciously, they understand how to choose between them—more precisely, they have "practical consciousness" but not "discursive consciousness" of the choice (Giddens, 1979, 1984). The lack of intentional individual action in making these choices makes the blaming of teachers or students problematic. Yet it might be quite reasonable for blame to be directed at the English Curriculum Branch of the Education Department. Conscious awareness of the distinction between the active and the passive voice is widespread throughout the branch because it is, after all, the job of the branch to attend to such matters and to raise the consciousness of teachers and students. It may thus make sense to lay collective blame for social action produced unintentionally, even unconsciously, by all the individual actors. Apart from the justice our campaigner may perceive in blaming the English Curriculum Branch rather than the students or teachers, she might conclude that change is more likely to be effected by collective blame. This raises the issue of collective action and deterrent efficacy, as discussed in the section after next.

Corporations Can Commit Crime

If we can accept that corporations have ethical and legal responsibilities, that corporations can act, and that corporations can be held blameworthy for their actions, then corporations can commit crime. We have also argued that corporate intentionality is a coherent idea, having both similarities to and differences from the idea of individual intentionality. But one does not have to believe in corporate intentionality, as Cressey suggests one does, in order to accept that corporations can commit crime. Intention is not the only basis for attributing fault for corporate action; further possible bases of corporate fault include recklessness, negligence, and "wilful blindness" (Wilson, 1979). There is no novelty in this point. With individuals, mens rea does not mean simply intention: it encompasses a panoply of fault concepts. Similarly, we have argued that it is unnecessary to accept the philosophically controversial idea that corporations are moral persons in order to justify holding corporations criminally responsible. Held puts this position nicely:

We seem to have some good reasons for conferring personhood on corporations, and some good reasons for denying it. I suggest that we sidestep the problem. It is not necessary to decide whether corporations "are" persons unless we have some unwarranted assumptions that only persons can act, or be responsible, or decide, etc. If what we are interested in is corporate behavior, we can suppose we are talking about an entity which is like a person in some respects and unlike a person in other respects. We can "hold" corporations responsible, in both moral and legal judgments. We can recognize that we need moralities that will recommend guidelines for the actions of corporations as we need guidelines for the actions of individual persons [1986:178].

Put another way, no modern society can afford a criminal law that communicates the message that, so long as we avoid individual fault, there is no need to worry about corporate fault. Equally, no society can afford a criminal law that communicates the message that, so long as the corporation is kept in the clear, we need not worry about individual fault on the part of actors in corporate roles. What is needed is a criminal law that inculcates both individual and corporate responsibility.

Corporations Can Suffer from Punishment

Cressey's critique here is that "criminologists rather routinely, unthinkingly and erroneously assert that corporations have the psychological capacity to be guilty of crime and to suffer from punishment" (1988:34). It is true that corporations have "no soul to damn, no body to kick." But contemporary social constructions of individual punishment do not generally involve the infliction of pain by causing bodies to bleed, nor do they involve the damning of souls. Rather they tend to involve the identification of individual goals—wealth, security, freedom—and the infliction of punishments that frustrate those goals. For example, the judge assumes that the defendant shares the goal of wealth accumulation when she imposes a fine; she assumes freedom to be desired when she imposes a sentence of imprisonment. From time to time these assumptions will be misplaced. First, there will be individuals who do not care for money or freedom. Second, and more fundamentally, doubt can be cast on the idea that human behavior is all about the pursuit of goals or interests. Equally, it can be about sustaining an identity or nurturing a self-concept as, say, a Christian or a lawyer, even when sustaining that identity is not in the interests of the actor.

Individual behavior can be understood in useful but limited ways both as a process of displaying and sustaining an identity (Bowles and Gintis, 1986) and as the pursuit of goals or interests. Equally, we would contend, corporate behavior can be usefully constructed both as a display of identity and the pursuit of goals. If individual and corporate conduct share in common at least some degree of goal-directedness, then it is just as sensible to seek to punish corporations by interfering with their goal attainment as it is to do so with individuals. Partial account of corporate action though it is, there is reason to believe that corporate crime better fits the model of rational goal seeking than does individual crime (Braithwaite and Geis, 1982).

If corporate behavior is partly about the attainment of collective goals, punishment of individuals alone is bound to fail as a control strategy. We must seek as well a capacity to interfere directly with those collective goals. This is so because if corporations rationally pursue goals, individuals who are deterred from following those goals on behalf of the corporation will be replaced by individuals who will pursue the corporate goals. Adherence to the individualist fallacy of division will have disastrous practical consequences for enforcement policy.

Let us try to make the point more clearly by comparing collective deterrence in the domain of foreign policy. Following Cressey, we could adopt the view that individuals, not nations, decide to go to war. Instead of threatening nuclear or commercial retaliation against a nation should it invade another, we could threaten to find out who the political actors were that lobbied for the invasion and to send assassination squads after them. This policy option is not usually recommended, largely because of an enduring belief in the capacity of groups to replace slain leaders. If collective deterrence is a fiction, it is a fiction on which strategic analysts in the United States and the Soviet Union have based the future of the world (Schelling, 1960; Kenny, 1985).

It is quite possible to deter by damaging collective interests even when individual members of an organization are not personally affected. In an earlier study of seventeen adverse publicity crises experienced by large organizations, we concluded that adverse publicity surrounding allegations of corporate crime was an effective deterrent, but not mainly because of fear of the financial consequences of the publicity (Fisse and Braithwaite, 1983). Companies value a good reputation for its own sake, just as do universities, sporting clubs, and government agencies. Individuals who take on positions of power within such organizations, even if they as individuals do not personally feel any deterrent effects of censure directed at their organization, may find that they confront role expectations to protect and enhance the repute of the organization. For example, an academic might be indifferent to the reputation of her university; indeed she might do more to snipe at the incompetence of the administration than to defend it publicly. But, if appointed as dean of a faculty, she confronts new role expectations that she will protect the university's reputation. She may do this diligently, not because of the views she brought to the job as an individual member of the university community, but because she knows what the position requires, and she wants to be good at her task. Thus, in organizations where individuals are stung very little by collective deterrents, deterrence can still work if those in power are paid good salaries on the understanding that they will do what is necessary to preserve the reputation of the organization or to protect it from whatever other kind of collective adversity is threatened.

The Same Theory Can Be Applied to Individual and Corporate Criminals

Cressey's ultimate concern is that the "blurring of the distinction between corporate crimes committed by persons and corporate crimes committed by organizations asks theoreticians to use one causal theory to explain both, an impossible task" (1988:40). This task is not impossible, though it does require negotiating a mine field of difficulties. In the last section, we concluded that models that conceive that crime is understandable in terms of rational pursuit of goals can have partial validity for both individual and corporate actors. Thus, there is a prospect of rational-choice models accounting for some variance with both types of criminal actors.

Corporations can learn, so there is the possibility of learning theory applying to both collectivities and individuals.

Just as individuals can participate in and be influenced by a subculture, so can corporations. Cressey's (1976) contribution on criminogenic corporate subcultures of restraint of trade, and the similarities of these to neighborhood subcultures of delinquency, is perhaps the most outstanding contribution to this literature. Corporate offending patterns, like individual offending patterns, may be accounted for by the configurations of legitimate and illegitimate opportunities that actors confront. Rational-choice, learning, subcultural, and opportunity theories doubtless do not exhaust the possibilities for theories that may apply to criminal action by both individual and collective entities. Equally, there are many theories of individual offending that it is difficult to see ever being usefully applied to corporations—such as biological theories of the relation between intelligence, impulsiveness, or race and crime.

The fundamental point is that it is impossible, in advance of a theory being developed and put to the test, to rule out any level of generality in theory application. Braithwaite, in chapter 8 of this volume, argues just this. As suggested there, before Darwin, the idea that the same theory could account for the origins of both man and amoebas was implausible. Criminology will not progress as a science if its practitioners suffer stultified creativity at the hands of an orthodoxy that theories of a certain scope are, to use Cressey's word, "impossible."

Conclusion

Cressey has done a service in his last published work. Sociologists are especially prone to the folly of treating nonactors as actors, as is evident from the sweeping flourishes often made about "the ruling class deciding," when no decision-making structures can be identified within an entity called the ruling class. Cressey's article puts all on guard against such all-too-common Type I errors. Our hope is that it will not also cause criminologists to perpetrate a host of Type II errors, discarding the reality of collective criminal action in favor of an inferior methodological individualism.

We wish to thank Gilbert Geis, Susan Shapiro, and Diane Vaughan for comments on earlier versions of this paper.

References

Bowles, Samuel, and Herbert Gintis. 1986. *Democracy and Capitalism.* New York: Basic Books.

Braithwaite, John. 1989. "The State of Criminology: Theoretical Decay or Renaissance." In *Advances in Criminological Theory,* vol. 2, edited by William S. Laufer and Freda Adler. New Brunswick, N.J.: Transaction Publishers.

Braithwaite, John, and Gilbert Geis. 1982. "On Theory and Action for Corporate Crime Control." *Crime and Delinquency* 28:292–316.

Bruns, N. 1985. "Corporate Preventive Law Programs." *Preventive Law Reporter* 6:30–40.

Colomy, Paul. 1988. "Donald R. Cressey: A Personal and Intellectual Remembrance." *Crime and Delinquency* 34:242–62.

Cooper, David. 1972. "Responsibility and the 'System'." In *Individual and Collective Responsibility: The Massacre at My Lai,* edited by Peter A. French. Cambridge, Mass.: Schenkman Publishing Company.

Cressey, Donald R. 1960. "Epidemiology and Individual Conduct: A Case from Criminology." *Pacific Sociological Review* 3:47–58.

———. 1976. "Restraint of Trade, Recidivism, and Delinquent Neighborhoods." In *Delinquency, Crime and Society,* edited by J. F. Short, Jr. Chicago: University of Chicago Press.

———. 1988. "The Poverty of Theory in Corporate Crime Research." *Advances in Criminological Theory* 1:31–56.

Dan-Cohen, Meir. 1986. *Rights, Persons, and Organizations.* Berkeley: University of California Press.

De George, Richard T. 1986. "Corporations and Morality." In *Shame, Responsibility and the Corporation,* edited by H. Curtler. New York: Haven Publications.

Donaldson, Thomas. 1982. *Corporations and Morality.* Englewood Cliffs: Prentice-Hall.

———. 1986. "Personalizing Corporate Ontology: The French Way." In *Shame, Responsibility and the Corporation,* edited by H. Curtler. New York: Haven Publications.

Durkheim, Emile. 1911. *De la Division du Travail.* New York: Free Press.

———. 1938. *The Rules of Sociological Method.* New York: Free Press, 1966.

Emery, Fred E. 1969. *Systems Thinking.* Harmondsworth: Penguin.

Fisse, Brent, and John Braithwaite. 1983. *The Impact of Publicity on Corporate Offenders.* Albany: State University of New York Press.

French, Peter A. 1984. *Collective and Corporate Responsibility.* New York: Columbia University Press.

———. 1986. "Principles of Responsibility, Shame, and the Corporation."

In *Shame, Responsibility and the Corporation*, edited by H. Curtler. New York: Haven Publications.

Geertz, Clifford. 1973. *The Interpretation of Cultures*. New York: Basic Books.

———. 1983. *Local Knowledge*. New York: Basic Books.

Giddens, Anthony. 1979. *Central Problems in Social Theory: Action, Structure, and Contradiction in Social Analysis*. London: Macmillan.

———. 1984. *The Construction of Society: Outline of the Theory of Structuration*. Berkeley: University of California Press.

Goffman, Erving. 1971. *Relations in Public*. New York: Basic Books.

Goodin, Robert E. 1987. "Apportioning Responsibility." *Law and Philosophy* 6:167–85.

Hayek, F. A. 1949. *Individualism and the Economic Order*. Chicago: University of Chicago Press.

Held, Virginia. 1986. "Corporations, Persons and Responsibility." In *Shame, Responsibility and the Corporation*, edited by H. Curtler. New York: Haven Publications.

Hindess, Barry. 1988. "Classes, Collectivities and Corporate Actors." Unpublished manuscript. Canberra: Australian National University.

Janis, Irving L. 1972. *Victims of Groupthink*. Boston: Houghton-Mifflin.

Janis, Irving L., and Leon Mann. 1977. *Decision Making: A Psychological Analysis of Conflict, Choice, and Commitment*. New York: Free Press.

Kenny, Anthony. 1985. *The Logic of Deterrence*. Chicago: University of Chicago Press.

Ladd, John. 1986. "Persons and Responsibility: Ethical Concepts and Impertinent Analyses." In *Shame, Responsibility and the Corporation*, edited by H. Curtler. New York: Haven Publications.

Laub, John H. 1983. *Criminology in the Making: An Oral History*. Boston: Northeastern University Press.

Lukes, Steven. 1973. *Individualism*. Oxford: Blackwell.

McDonald, Michael. 1987. "The Personless Paradigm." *University of Toronto Law Journal* 37:212–26.

May, Larry. 1983. "Vicarious Agency and Corporate Responsibility." *Philosophical Studies* 43:82.

———. 1986. "Negligence and Corporate Criminality." In *Shame, Responsibility and the Corporation*, edited by H. Curtler. New York: Haven Publications.

Popper, Karl. 1947. *The Open Society and its Enemies*. London: Routledge.

Schelling, Thomas C. 1960. *The Strategy of Conflict*. Cambridge: Harvard University Press.

Sciamanda, J. 1987. "Preventive Law Leads to Corporate Goal of Zero Litigation, Zero Legal Violations." *Preventive Law Reporter* 6:3–8.

Shaver, K. G. 1985. *The Attribution of Blame: Causality, Responsibility and Blameworthiness*. New York: Springer-Verlag.

Simon, Herbert. 1965. *Administrative Behavior*. 2nd ed. New York: Free Press.

Surber, J. 1983. "Individual and Corporate Responsibility: Two Alternative Approaches." *Business and Professional Ethics Journal* 2:67–88.

Thompson, Paul B. 1986. "Why Do We Need a Theory of Corporate Responsibility?" In *Shame, Responsibility and the Corporation*, edited by H. Curtler. New York: Haven Publications.

Wallach, M. A., N. Kogan, and D. J. Bem. 1964. "Diffusion of Responsibility and Level of Risk Taking in Groups." *Journal of Abnormal and Social Psychology* 68:263–74.

Walter, C., and E. P. Richards. 1986. "Corporate Counsel's Role in Risk Minimization: Lessons from Bhopal." *Preventive Law Reporter* 4:139–54.

Wilson, Larry C. 1979. "The Doctrines of Wilful Blindness." *University of New Brunswick Law Journal* 28:175–94.

Wittgenstein, Ludwig. 1975. *Philosophical Remarks*. Oxford: Blackwell.

3

Parental Work Control and Delinquency: A Theoretical and Empirical Critique

Raymond Paternoster and Charles R. Tittle

Introduction

Numerous complaints in the crime and delinquency literature that extant theories are unnecessarily narrow in scope have provoked a movement toward theoretical synthesis of divergent theories (Elliott, 1985; Groves and Sampson, 1987; Liska, Krohn, and Messinger, 1989; Tittle, 1985; but see Bohm, 1987; Hirschi, 1979, for contrary positions), and some scholars have already formulated more general theories that attempt to incorporate the explanatory principles or processes postulated by separate, more theoretically restricted perspectives (see Conger, 1976; Elliott, Ageton and Johnson, 1979; Krohn, 1986; Wilson and Herrnstein, 1985; Cohen and Machalek, 1988). Perhaps the most provocative and ambitious of these attempts is the recent work by Mark Colvin and John Pauly (1983), who link the ideas of structural Marxist thinkers such as Erik Olin Wright (1978, 1979) and Richard Edwards (1979) with the organizational theory of Amitai Etzioni (1970), the theory of social bonding by Travis Hirschi (1969), and Richard Cloward and Lloyd Ohlin's modification of anomie theory (1960). Their integrated formulation blends macro and micro explanations to produce a unified "structural-Marxist theory of delinquency production."

In this paper we offer a logical and empirical critique of the Colvin/Pauly theory. We contend that it is almost certainly incorrect in its basic assumptions and its consequent predictions, and that it incorporates a number of logical and practical difficulties that make it scientifically untenable. Our critique is a sympathetic one, however. We believe that the theoretical integration movement is useful—indeed, essential—for scientific development in the field of criminology, and we admire and commend Colvin and Pauly for their effort. However, since their formulation appeared in a leading journal and could be regarded as an exemplar of integrated theory (see papers in Liska, Krohn, and Messinger, 1989), we feel compelled to highlight its defects, lest the integration movement be falsely judged by an inadequate benchmark. Moreover, we believe that future efforts to build synthetic theory will profit from careful attention to the problems that Colvin and Pauly encountered. It is inevitable that early efforts at a complex task will produce crude and often unworkable solutions. But progress can only be made if the errors of pioneering work are identified and avoided by others. Thus, we want to make it clear from the beginning that we accord Colvin and Pauly's work the greatest respect and that we view our critique as a constructive endeavor.

Our observations are oriented around three major focuses: (1) empirical application, (2) conceptual ambiguity, and (3) the congruence between simple hypotheses suggested by the model and available (though limited) empirical data.

The Theory

The basic thesis of the Colvin/Pauly theory is that serious patterned delinquency (defined by them (p. 513) as "repeated engagement of a juvenile in the FBI's Part One Index crimes") is the ultimate product of the social relations engendered by particular positions within advanced capitalist production. But despite its structural grounding, the actual process through which capitalist social relations generate particular forms of delinquency is said to be a social psychological one. Like all structural Marxists (Braverman, 1974; Edwards, 1979; Wright, 1978, 1979), Colvin and Pauly describe the class division of advanced industrial capitalist society in relation to the ownership of the means or ends of production (p.

526). They contend that modern capitalist society is roughly divided into two modes of production, capitalist and petty commodity production. The capitalist mode of production produces two major class divisions, the capitalist class and the working class. There are minor subclass divisions within these, however, for the capitalist class is divided into monopoly-sector capitalists, competitive-sector capitalists, and small employers. The working class is similarly divided into three "Fractions." Fraction I workers are those employed in competitive industries and engaged in low skill, nonunion, and menial jobs (examples: southern textile workers, agricultural wage-labor, service jobs) and those partially un- and underemployed persons described as "floating and surplus populations." Fraction II workers are predominantly made up of unionized industrial workers, while Fraction III workers include technical staff employees, salaried professionals, state employees, and wage-earning skilled manual workers (such as building-trade workers). Petty commodity production is, in turn, divided into the petty bourgeoisie and nonwage workers.

The beginning point of Colvin and Pauly's theory is the notion that workers are subjected to qualitatively different kinds of control structures within different classes and subclasses. Within the working class, for example, Fraction I workers are subjected to what Colvin and Pauly (after Etzioni, 1970) refer to as "simple control," or a *coercive compliance structure,* which includes dismissal from the job as the primary labor disciplinary tool. Fraction II workers, however, are subjected to a more *utilitarian control structure,* which relies on the manipulation of extrinsic rewards of material security (pay increments, steps up the seniority ladder) to shape worker compliance. Compliance from more independent Fraction III workers is obtained through what Colvin and Pauly call (p. 534) a *normative compliance structure,* which "rests on the allocation and manipulation of rewards" (Etzioni, 1970:104) and elicits a more moral, intrinsic commitment by the worker.

Experiencing these workplace controls creates for each worker a social-psychological orientation to authority, what Colvin and Pauly (p. 513–14) call "an ideological orientation for the individual in relation to the agents and apparatuses of social control." Being subject to coercive control structures, for instance, tends to create an alienated, or intense negative bond between the worker and "authority apparatuses." Employees in Fraction III jobs, by contrast, are exposed to normative compliance schemes that foster positive bonds between the worker, the employer, and the organization. Workplace controls that are mainly utilitarian (those on Fraction II workers) shape an ideological orientation that is calculative, and is both less intense than the other two and more tenuous since these controls depend "on continual remuneration and advancement up the pay ladder and produc[e] little loyalty on the part of the worker." According to Colvin and Pauly, then, objective class position, as defined by one's access to the mode and means of production, shapes a particular social-psychological state, a worker's "ideological orientation" toward work and authority.

The connection between class position, orientation toward workplace "authority apparatuses," and serious delinquency lies in the tendency for workers to recreate within the family the type of control structure they experience at work. Colvin and Pauly note that parents consciously or unconsciously communicate to their children messages about the world, specifically, that authorities are to be obeyed either out of external compulsion (fear or utilitarian calculation) or internalized and normative commitment. Fraction I parents, subject to coercive and obvious forms of control at the workplace, are hypothesized to be inconsistent in their use of discipline, oscillating between physical harshness and laxity. Fraction II parents, who experience less coercive and more utilitarian kinds of controls at work, are said to employ similarly calculative disciplinary techniques within the family. Finally, the more "self-directed" Fraction III parents tend to rely on pleas to conscience in order to discipline their children. As was true for workplace controls, experiences with different family controls are said to produce qualitatively different ideological bonds between parents and children. Those in coercively controlling families develop intensely negative ("alienated") bonds to one another, those in utilitarian controlling families form bonds of "intermediate intensity," and those experiencing normative control develop "positive bonds of high intensity" (Colvin and Pauly, 1983:536).

The next causal link in the chain of Colvin and Pauly's theory is that between family control structure (and type and strength of bond) and consequent control within the school and peer group. They hold that children who experience coercive controls within the family are more likely to be placed in a similar situation at school because negatively bonded children score lower on IQ and aptitude tests, and because they give off "behavioral cues of being . . . potentially disruptive" (p. 537). These coercive school control structures take the form of educational tracks. Furthermore, since friendship networks at school reflect proximity, those students in the lower (non–college preparatory) tracks are more likely to associate in groups with peers who have similarly negative bonds to school and family. Such peer groups in turn focus on and reinforce negative bonds, which, Colvin and Pauly contend, are conducive to involvement in serious, patterned delinquency. On the other hand, those students who come from families with moderately intensive, calculative bonds and those from families that foster intensive, normative, and positive bonds are more likely to be tracked into less coercive modes at school and form friendship cliques with similar kinds of control structures and bonds. These peer groups are far less likely to lead to the kind of serious, repeated involvement in delinquency that the coercively oriented peer structure does. Figure 3.1 is illustrative of the model of the capitalist production of delinquency as presented by Colvin and Pauly.

The Critique

Empirical Application

No matter how appealing or elegant a theory, it must be applicable to the real world if it is to be useful. Indeed, within a scientific context it must be capable of generating hypotheses that can be tested empirically to ascertain the theory's viability as a mechanism for understanding the phenomena to which it is addressed (not all regard criminological work as an appropriate object for scientific work, of course; see Bohm, 1987). Furthermore, when a theory proposes a series of causal connections constituting a process through which some variable (or variables) produces an ultimate outcome, as the Colvin/Pauly formulation does, it is important to be able to empirically evaluate the causal structure of the complete model. As we will show, it is possible to derive some hypotheses from the Colvin/Pauly theory that logically ought to be testable, but it may be impossible to test these crucial hypotheses satisfactorily

FIGURE 3.1

Reproduction of Colvin/Pauley's General Path Model of Patterned Delinquency

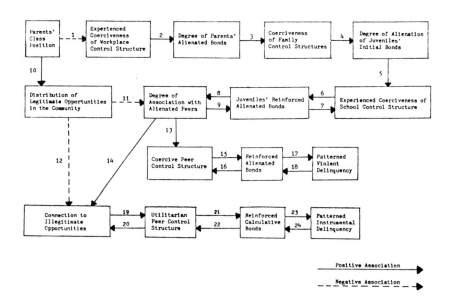

because of measurement difficulties stemming from conceptual ambiguities in the theory. Moreover, it is clearly not possible to estimate the complete causal model expressing the processual structure of the theoretical scheme, at least not as it is originally stated (see figure 3.1).

Inspection of figure 3.1 reveals only one completely exogenous variable (Parents' Objective Class Position), thirteen intervening, endogenous variables, and two purely endogenous variables (Patterned Violent Delinquency and Patterned Instrumental Delinquency). These variables are embedded in a causal process that in its simplest and most restrictive form includes seven reciprocal effects. With so many feedback relationships, the theoretical model is grossly underidentified, such that unique estimates of the proposed effects are impossible (Hanushek and Jackson, 1977; Heise, 1975). Moreover, Colvin and Pauly provide extremely limited insight about other exogenous (instrumental) variables that might be brought into their model to meet identification requirements, strangely suggesting that one such variable would be a traditionally conceived measure of socio-economic status (SES).[1]

Thus it is clear that even if the theory were otherwise flawless, it would still be incomplete. Much theoretical work remains to be done before scholars can even begin to apply the model empirically. This additional theorizing must specify other influences on key endogenous variables in the scheme, especially those that might affect one of each pair of reciprocal variables but not the other. But given the complexity of the model, including as it does numerous reciprocal effects, such work will not come easy. This is particularly true because Colvin and Pauly also postulate several conditional relationships, making estimation extremely difficult with traditional linear techniques, even if the model were identifiable.

As if this were not troublesome enough, the model, even in its current incomplete form, is probably mis-specified because it ignores other theoretically plausible effects, particularly other direct effects among the endogenous variables. For example, although Colvin and Pauly do not suggest a direct effect from "Coerciveness of Family Control Structures" to either "Coercive Peer Control Structure" or to "Patterned Delinquency" all of these effects, as well as many others, can be hypothesized from their presented theoretical discussion. If, as Colvin and Pauly contend, control structures "get into" the personalities of people through their effects on social bonds to the family, the resulting attitudes and behaviors should also have direct effects on other attitudes and behaviors focused on similar control structures in other social contexts, as well as on the propensity to commit various kinds of delinquency. This logically may be a second, related process through which control structures experienced in one realm of life are recreated in another. Thus, although the model is already quite complex, realistically it is probably far too simplistic.

Hence, the Colvin/Pauly model as a whole is simply not testable. Of course, current overall nontestability may not necessarily be a fatal flaw—as long as it is logically possible to test some parts of the scheme and to look forward to a time when more effective methods are available for evaluating the total structure. In this case one can derive specific, potentially testable hypotheses from various parts of the model. For example, we could, as a first step, simply postulate that Parents' Objective Class Position will be related to the probability of Patterned Violent Delinquency, initially ignoring the intervening links. After all, no matter what the mediating process, we would expect the initial independent variable to at least predict the last variable in the model beyond simple chance. And numerous other hypotheses could similarly be formulated. Unfortunately, however, the Colvin/Pauly theory contains so many conceptual ambiguities that it becomes almost impossible to measure the appropriate variables to test even the simpler, straightforward hypotheses that might be derived logically.

Conceptual Ambiguity

Although none of the variables in the theory are precisely defined, several of the key theoretical constructs are actually so poorly conceived that any meaningful measurement may be precluded. The three most important variables in the theory are (1) the primary endogenous variable, workplace control; (2) the eventual outcome variable, serious, patterned violent and property delinquency; and (3) the intervening variable, parent-child bonds.

Consider first the primary causative variable, workplace control. Colvin and Pauly identify three qualitatively distinct types of workplace control: (1) simple coercion, exemplified in a threat of dismissal from the job; (2) utilitarian control, reflected in the granting or withholding of material rewards such as wages and seniority; and (3) manipulative control, involving "an elaborate manipulation of symbols and statuses." This sounds simple enough until one contemplates how to measure workplace control. Colvin and Pauly do not say whether their theory concerns the factors that *actually* control behavior in a given situation, or whether it concerns the factors that are *intended* by employers to produce that effect. Moreover, they do not distinguish between *objective* characteristics of work situations and characteristics that are *perceived* by workers to be operative.

If we focus on the factors that actually produce conformity in a workplace we will discover that identifying such forces is itself an enormous undertaking, entailing a series of complex studies or experiments that may not, in fact, produce the desired knowledge. Research on the deterrence question (see Gibbs, 1975 and Paternoster, 1987 for reviews) suggests it may not be possible to ascertain what actually influences behavior in a workplace (or anyplace else), much less measure it. If one cannot establish the cause of conformity, how can one measure the degree to which the conformity-causing variable exists in a given work setting?

Nevertheless, as difficult as it would be to identify and measure the actual controlling elements in a work situation, it would at least become a reasonable goal if we could be sure that that is what is implied by the Colvin/Pauly formulation. Unfortunately we don't know what the theory implies. Suppose, for example, that we decide to look at employer records to determine what happened in the past when an employee of the type in question began to do poorly on the job, and suppose we find that in most instances the worker had been fired. But suppose we also do a survey of the workers and learn that most of them do not fear being fired (some conform because of a work ethic, some think their own poor work will not be discovered, some think they are extra lucky). Could we conclude that this workplace was coercively controlled such that all the workers would be expected to form alienated bonds and recreate the same situation in their families? Suppose, on the other hand, that we examine those employer records and find that most discovered cases of poor work had resulted in reprimand rather than firing, but that a survey indicated that most of the workers *believed* they would be fired if they did poor work. Could we say this workplace is coercively controlled? Further, if employer records indicated high probability of firing for poor work and most workers believed they would be fired, could we conclude that it was this actual and/or perceived coercion that shaped behavior among the workers? Might not it be possible that other factors produce the conformity to work standards even though sanctions are a realistic and perceived reality? Finally, suppose the usual practice is for poor workers to be fired and that most workers thought they would be fired, but a survey revealed that most perceived that their own conformity was motivated by something besides fear of job loss. Would this be a coercively controlled work place? The point is that the concept is too ambiguous and imprecise to permit careful tests of even the most straightforward hypotheses.

The problem of ambiguous concepts and consequent problems of measurement becomes even larger when we look at the other two main variables. Colvin and Pauly emphatically state that theirs is a model designed to explain "serious patterned delinquent behavior, defined as *repeated engagement of a juvenile in the FBI's Part One Index crimes*" (p. 513, emphasis added). In another place they again firmly state that the dependent variable is "sustained involvement in serious delinquency" (p. 539). And they reinforce this point when they discuss extant research using self-report indicators in studying the relationship between delinquency and social class (p. 515), faulting it because of inadequate measures of both class position and delinquency. They particularly criticize self-reports that "fail to tap significant differences in frequency and seriousness of delinquent behavior." And they go on to say that previously undocumented class-delinquency relationships will emerge once the focus is on sustained involvement in serious delinquent behavior. Thus, on one hand a reader is led to believe that Colvin and Pauly are interested in explaining the *frequency* of serious acts of delinquency among the subgroup of those who are serious delinquents, and conversely that the model is not intended to explain *why* some young persons become serious offenders in the first place.

Consistent with this theme, Colvin and Pauly suggest that ideological bonds vary by the *degree* of coercion employed in the relevant control structure; that is, within each context (work, family, school, and peer group) affective bonds may be arrayed on a continuum from intensely negative to intensely positive, depending upon the amount of coercion inherent in the structure of the particular context. Thus, speaking of the family:

> The more coercive this structure of control, the more negative are the bonds produced in the child. The *degree of coerciveness* of family control structures is influenced by material resources available to parents as reinforcements and by the ideological bond of the parent [p. 535, emphasis added].

The connection between the intervening variable of family control and the outcome variable of serious, patterned delinquency, and the apparent gist of the theory, is expressed in the following statement:

The more coercive the control relations encountered in these various socialization contexts [work, family, school, peer groups] tend to be, the more negative or alienated will be the individual's ideological bond and the more likely is the individual to engage in serious, patterned delinquency. We agree with Etzioni that coercive controls create an alienative orientation to authority. They create negative bonds and open the individual to entry into peer associations that reinforce patterned delinquent behavior [p. 515].

So far, so good. Even though such a theory is exceptionally narrow, focusing, as it seems to, only on serious, repeated delinquency, which constitutes less than 3 percent of delinquent behavior (Hagan, Gills, and Sampson, 1985), it would at least be empirically applicable. If Colvin and Pauly had left it at that, we could proceed to try to measure coerciveness of control structures, amount of alienation in social bonds, and frequency of serious delinquency using scales or indexes that express degrees of the different variables on numerical continuums and then observe (measure) the predicted associations among the variables so measured.

Unfortunately, the theorists muddy the waters by simultaneously arguing that the theory is about *types* of delinquency rather than frequency of offending, by simultaneously suggesting that ideological bonds to authority vary according to *type,* rather than along a single continuum of "coerciveness." Thus when they note the importance of Etzioni's discussion of different types of compliance for their own model, they state:

Our analysis borrows heavily from Etzioni's (1970) compliance theory, which postulates a relationship between the *type of power* employed for control (normative, remunerative, or coercive) and the *type of subordinate's ideological involvement* in compliance relationships (moral, calculative, or alienative) [Colvin and Pauly, 1983:514, emphasis added].

Contrary to the previously described argument, this suggests that control structures do not really vary by degrees according to the extent to which they are coercive, but must instead be categorized according to type. And it suggests that ideological bonds do not vary along a dimension of positive to negative or nonalienating to alienating, but are classed according to qualitatively different, non-ordered types.

Continuing with this alternative theme of qualitative distinctions among types of control structures and ideological orientations to authority, Colvin and Pauly hypothesize that these variations are related to the *probability of involvement in different types of delinquency* rather than the frequency of involvement in serious delinquent behavior:

> Our specific concern is with structures of control that solicit and compel certain types of behavior from individuals and shape an ideological orientation for the individual in relation to the agents and apparatuses of social control [p. 513].

Furthermore, in discussing the specifics of their delinquency model, they emphatically state that the type of bond experienced by youths in different contexts is causally related to the type of delinquency they are likely to participate in:

> Depending on the interaction between specific internal structures of control within delinquent groups and specific external structures of opportunity in the surrounding environment, the delinquent peer groups will produce either instrumental or violent patterned delinquent behavior [p. 542].

Specifically, Colvin and Pauly hypothesize that coercive control structures foster alienating/negative bonds, which "propel these juveniles into serious, patterned, *violent delinquent behavior*" (p. 543, emphasis in original), while utilitarian control structures produce a more calculative bond which "propels these juveniles into serious, patterned, *instrumental delinquent behavior*" (p. 543, emphasis in original).

Therefore, Colvin and Pauly contradict their previously described theorizing by suggesting that work-control structures, and the consequent ideological bonds to authority they produce, are all discrete variables, reflecting nonordered types, with a distinct type of social context producing a propensity for a distinct type of delinquency. This conceptual ambiguity not only weakens the theoretical argument, but it makes it almost impossible to measure the variables for empirical test—even if the hypothesis to be tested is straightforward rather than embedded in a complex causal process. If the variables are at once linear and continuous as well as discrete and typological, then it follows that measurement must capture more or less pure differentiated "types" within various ranges of an actual continuum. For example, the concept of ideological bonds must be conceived as involving qualitative differences in bonding (alienative, calculative, normative) that can nevertheless be arrayed on a quantitative continuum with "negative bonds equaling alienated involvement, intermediate bonds equaling calculative involvement, and positive bonds equaling moral involvement" (p. 519, n. 3). But Colvin and Pauly provide no specifics as to how this kind of measurement can be done with their variables, and, to our knowledge, there is no literature concerning such a method. Indeed, despite repeated efforts with a variety of currently available scaling and/or index-construction techniques, we were unable to generate measurements that simultaneously express the *degree* of affect a child has for his or her family and the *nature* of the relationship between parent and child.

One practical solution to this measurement problem might be simply to ignore the contradictions inherent in the Colvin/Pauly argument and employ a linear-based measurement and estimation strategy that assumes the key variables are to be *degrees* of coercion, alienation, and serious delinquency. But to do so would violate several fundamental premises on which the theory is presumably based. Indeed, despite the emphases about linearity noted earlier, and despite the pictorial display that suggests a continuous variable model, Colvin and Pauly actually stress the discrete, typological version of their argument.

Therefore, a second, and probably more faithful, solution would be to ignore their linear argument altogether and focus completely on a discrete variable approach. To do this, one might test hypotheses, or estimate the model, three separate times, using on each trial discrete dichotomous measures of all the variables. For instance, on trial one the measure of violent delinquency might be a two-value indicator—the juvenile commits violent delinquency or he or she doesn't (he or she either commits no delinquency or commits some other type). The measure of control structure might similarly be a dichotomy—the individual experiences coercive control or he or she doesn't (he or she experiences one of the other types or no control at all). A test would then be performed and repeated using, for the second trial, a dichotomous measure of delinquency—the juvenile does instrumental delinquency or he or she doesn't (he or she does some other type of delinquency or no delinquency at all)—and dichotomous measures of the other variables, such as type of control—the individual experiences calculative control or he or she doesn't (he or she experiences some other kind of control or none at all). And so on for the third trial, where the outcome is a dichotomy of no delinquency versus any type of delinquency.

But if the variables are taken to be discrete types of controls, ideological bonds, and delinquency, as in this example, and as implied by the predominant theme of the Colvin/Pauly theory, then two additional and potentially more problematic difficulties emerge. First of all, this version implies that youths experience only specific types of controls and bonds that do not change over the life cycle nor vary by disciplinary occasion and are exclusive with regard to other types of controls and bonds (once some cut point has been decided in order to classify individuals as having been controlled in the family in one fashion or another). Fraction I workers, who are presumably exposed to coercive control structures on the job, will, then, re-create a fixed type of control structure (coercive) within the family, that does not change over time (presuming that they remain within that class). Similarly, Fraction III employees, who experience normative controls at work, must unvaryingly reproduce a normative type of disciplinary technique with their children, regardless of their ages, genders, or the disciplinary situation. Correspondingly, those discrete control structures (and consequent discrete bonds) in the family must produce an exclusive type of delinquency, either instrumental or violent.

Congruence with Empirical Data

These two assumptions, that parental disciplinary practices are defined by class position and invariant with respect to situational vagaries (occasion, age, gender, etc.) and that involvement in delinquent behavior is specialized and exclusive, are inconsistent with most empirical data.

Invariance of parental disciplinary techniques. Evidence in existing literature, as well as our own data collected to examine this issue, indicates that parental use of coercive controls cuts across class distinctions, and varies by gender and age of the child as well as by the specific situation that calls forth parental efforts at discipline. In his study of SES variations in attitudes and behavior, for example, Kohn, whose work provides strong input into the Colvin/Pauly theory, reports that class differences in the use of coercive punishments are slight, and vary more by the *situations* of its use:

One cannot conclude that mothers of either social class are quick to employ coercion. But when children *persist* in wild play, fights with brothers or sisters, or in displays of temper, both middle- and working-class mothers are likely to turn to one or another form of punishment. . . . It would seem, then, that the difference between middle- and working-class mothers' use of physical punishment is not in the frequency with which they use it, but in the conditions under which they use it [1969:95, emphasis in original].

Thus Kohn's data suggest that physical punishment is not the sanction of first resort for parents of any social class, but is instead reserved for serious situations:

Neither middle- nor working-class parents resort to punishment as a first recourse when children misbehave. . . . [B]ut when children persist in misbehavior, despite parents' attempts to forestall them, parents are likely to resort to one or another form of coercion.

And Kohn found that the coerciveness of punishment declines with the age of the child: "As the children grow older . . . fathers become progressively less likely to use physical punishment no matter what the situation" (1969:103).

Because the assumption that workplace control, which is supposedly class linked, is translated into social control in the family is so crucial to the Colvin/Pauly theory, we decided to collect additional information about that presumed relationship. We asked a sample of high school students (n = 1,076) in the twelfth grade to report the predominant type of disciplinary method used on them by their parents on those occasions when the juvenile did something of which the parents disapproved.[2] We also asked them to report the disciplinary methods used by their parents on them five years earlier. This produced data concerning parental disciplinary techniques for youth approximately seventeen years of age as well as the disciplinary techniques used on those same children when they were twelve years of age (at least as perceived by the youth). In keeping with Colvin and Pauly's characterization, parental discipline was classified as coercive if the student reported he or she was "physically punished" or "sometimes physically punished and sometimes nothing would happen"; it was categorized as of a calculative type if the student said that he or she "would have lost some privileges"; and normative if he or she "would have been shamed, or would have been made to feel guilty." The results are reported in tables 3.1, 3.2, and 3.3.

As shown, overall there is only a modest degree of stability in the punishment techniques employed by parents as children grow older. Furthermore, the observed instability does not appear to be random, but follows the pattern that Kohn (1969) found in his earlier study. This can be observed in several ways. First, the diagonal elements of table 3.1 indicate that only a little over one-half of our sample (55 percent) reported that the type of parental discipline currently used is the same as it was five years ago.

TABLE 3.1
Type of Parental Discipline
(Employed on Children While Seniors in High School and Five Years Before That)

Disciplinary Type Five Years Ago	CURRENT DISCIPLINARY TYPE			
	Coercive	Calculative	Normative	Total
Coercive	113	221	74	408 (37%)
Calculative	55	400	104	559 (51%)
Normative	6	34	85	125 (11%)
Total	174	655	263	1,092
	(16%)	(60%)	(24%)	

Gamma = .46

Moreover the direction of change in disciplinary technique among the 45 percent who experienced change was mainly away from coercive control and toward greater use of calculative and normative methods as the child grew older. This can be seen clearly in table 3.2, a transition matrix for these students of punishment types from five years ago to the currently employed method. Only 28 percent of the students who were coercively disciplined five years earlier are still disciplined that way, while 72 percent of the calculatively and 68 percent of the normatively disciplined continue to be so handled by their parents. Thus 45 percent (494) of all the students experienced a change in parental discipline techniques over the five year period, but 60 percent (295) of those changes were shifts in parental discipline style from coercive to one of the others, while only 12 percent (61) of the shifts are from one of the other two types toward coercivity. Yet our data show almost no change in objective class position of those who could be classified as working class.

It is also the case that the type of disciplinary technique employed by parents in this sample is different for male and female children. Table 3.3 shows the kind of discipline employed by parents of both genders at the two points in time. At age twelve the males were substantially more likely to be punished coercively than were females (43 percent versus 31 percent). And, consistent with our other findings, both males and females were much less likely to be punished coercively when seniors in high school than they were earlier in life. But again we have no evidence that the fathers of the males were more likely to be in one fraction of the working class than were the fathers of females.

In sum, both the extent and pattern of change in disciplinary technique observed here call into question the core assumption of

TABLE 3.2
Transition Matrix for Changes in Parental Disciplinary Techniques
(Currently Employed vs Employed Five Years Ago)

Disciplinary Type Five Years Ago	CURRENT DISCIPLINARY TYPE		
	Coercive	Calculative	Normative
Coercive	.277	.542	.181
Calculative	.098	.716	.186
Normative	.048	.272	.680

TABLE 3.3
Type of Parental Discipline of Males vs. Females
(Employed on Children While Seniors in High School and Five Years Before That)

| | CURRENT DISCIPLINARY TYPE | | | |
	Coercive	Calculative	Normative	Total
Males	108	349	116	573
	(18.8%)	(60.9%)	(20.2%)	
Females	69	306	147	522
	(13.2%)	(58.6%)	(28.2%)	
	DISCIPLINARY TYPE FIVE YEARS AGO			
	Coercive	Calculative	Normative	Total
Males	246	271	55	573
	(43.0%)	(47.4%)	(9.6%)	
Females	163	288	70	522
	(31.3%)	(55.3%)	(13.4%)	

Colvin and Pauly's theoretical model—that parental controls are an invariant function of parents' social class position. The data exhibited above, as well as that reported by Kohn (1969), suggests that the type of discipline used by parents is at least partially a function of the age and sex of the child.

Delinquency specialization. If the second key theoretical proposition of the Colvin/Pauly scheme is true; that is, if *types* of control structure are related to *types* of delinquency, then there should be great similarity in the kinds of offenses delinquents commit over time. Colvin and Pauly specifically hypothesize (p. 543) that coercive compliance structures are conducive to violent delinquency while (through an independent process) calculative compliance methods facilitate involvement in instrumental (property) delinquencies, and they suggest that because of the different causal mechanisms at work, commission of these offense types will be mutually exclusive:

Depending on the interaction between specific internal structures of control within delinquent groups and specific external controls of opportunity in the surrounding environment, the delinquent peer groups will produce *either* instrumental or violent patterned delinquent behavior [p. 542, emphasis added].

Therefore we should find that serious property offenders specialize in property offenses and that violent offenders commit mainly (if not exclusively) violent offenses.

The evidence, however, indicates that most delinquents, even those who are involved in serious offenses, are nonspecialists in their offending patterns. Tables 3.4 and 3.5 are transition matrixes summarizing the findings about offense specialization from the most complete cohort data available (Wolfgang, Figlio, and Sellin, 1972; Wolfgang, Thornberry, and Figlio, 1987). They show the probability of a juvenile offender being arrested for a particular type of crime, given the type of the previous offense for which he was arrested. If juveniles specialize in their delinquencies we would expect the largest probabilities to be in the diagonal cells, indicating, for example, that those who were previously arrested for an offense involving an injury were most likely to be arrested for another

Table 3.4
Summary Transition Matrix
(All Offenders, First to Eighth Transitions)

k-1/k	Nonindex	Injury	Theft	Damage	Combi-nation	Desist
Nonindex	.4473	.0685	.1054	.0228	.0492	.3068
Injury	.4090	.0920	.0854	.0222	.0600	.3314
Theft	.4051	.0530	.2130	.0235	.0929	.2126
Damage	.5013	.0882	.1463	.0529	.0343	.1770
Combination	.3922	.0703	.1378	.0169	.1350	.2478
Desist	.0000	.0000	.0000	.0000	.0000	1.0000

Source: Wolfgang, Figlio, and Sellin, 1972:183.

TABLE 3.5
Transition Probabilities
(All Offenders, Eighth Transition)

k-l/k	N	Nonindex	Injury	Theft	Damage	Combi-nation	Desist
Nonindex	166	.5060	.1084	.1145	.0241	.0663	.1807
Injury	30	.4667	.0333	.0667	.0000	.1000	.3333
Theft	53	.4906	.0377	.2075	.0189	.1132	.1320
Damage	6	.6667	.1667	.1667	.0000	.0000	.0000
Combination	27	.2593	.1111	.0741	.0000	.1852	.3703
Total	282						

Source: Wolfgang, Figlio, and Sellin, 1972:178.

injury offense. The tables, however, do not show that. Those arrested for an injury-incurring index offense (violence) were more likely to be arrested for a nonindex offense as their next delinquency than for another violent crime (.4090 versus .0920; see table 3.4).

The evidence is somewhat more supportive of the idea that some delinquents specialize primarily in instrumental or property offenses, but even here the indications are modest at best. Those who were arrested for a property offense (theft) were much more likely to be arrested for a nonindex offense the next time (p = .4051) than they were to be arrested for another index theft (p = .2130): about twice as likely. Thus, if arrest data are indicative, there is greater specialization with property delinquencies, but certainly it cannot be said that delinquents show any great degree of concentration of their offenses even on property crimes. In fact, it should be noted that table 3.4 demonstrates that the typical offender in the Philadelphia cohort was most likely to be arrested for a nonindex offense the next time, and after that was more likely to *cease offending* (not be arrested again) than he was to commit any other delinquent act (see Wolfgang, Figlio, and Sellin, 1972:189).

However, since Colvin and Pauly are concerned only with frequent offending, it might be argued that only repeat, "hardcore" delinquents would exhibit specialization in offending patterns, a phenomenon that might be obscured in data such as that presented in table 3.4, which includes all cohort delinquents. But even if we focus only on that smaller subset arrested for the ninth time, we reach the same conclusion. Table 3.5 allows one to ask, "given that the eighth arrest is for 'crime x,' what is the probability that the next arrest will also be for 'crime x'?" Those delinquents who were arrested for an injury-incurring index offense for their eighth delinquency were most likely to be arrested next for a nonindex offense (p = .4667). In fact they were twice as likely to be arrested for a subsequent theft offense as they were for an injury-related crime (p's = .0667 and .0333, respectively), and the conditional probability that the ninth arrest would be for an injury offense, given that the eight arrest was also for an injury offense, was actually less (.0333) than the nonconditional probability of an injury incurring arrest (.0886).[3] As before, those arrested for theft were more likely to be arrested for another theft than they were for another index offense; the conditional probability that the ninth arrest would be for a theft, given the fact that the eighth arrest was also for a theft (.2075) was almost twice (.2130) the nonconditional probability of a theft occurring (.1241). But again, even this much specialization is quite modest, since the most likely next arrest for previous theft arrestees was for a nonindex delinquency. Thus these and other data[4] suggest that delinquent offending is not particularly specialized. This would appear to cast considerable doubt on the Colvin/Pauly theory—at least on the discrete, typological version that appears to be their main focus.

Questionable Causal Links

We previously argued that the Colvin/Pauly causal model as a whole could not be tested but that some specific hypotheses might be derived and empirically evaluated, provided certain measurement problems could be handled. Here we derive two such hypotheses and offer tests based on one solution to the measurement dilemma. We regard these two hypotheses as crucial to the entire theory; if they prove untenable, then it is extremely unlikely that the overall model would have much value.

The most important causal links in the Colvin/Pauly scheme are at the front end, involving putative effects of parental work-control structures on methods used in the family context to discipline children and the effects of family control structure on the parent-child bond that comes to embody the "ideological orientation" to authority. Recall that Colvin and Pauly claim that coercive controls faced in the workplace are re-created within the family, and that it is these coercive family controls that provide the indirect links to serious patterned delinquency. What is truly unique about this theory, then, is its assertion that social class is related to delinquency through its influence on child management techniques employed within the family. If workplace controls are actually unrelated to family control, and if coercive family controls are not associated with negative, alienated bonds, one would have no basis for presuming the validity of the remainder of the model, which links alienated family bonds to control structures in the school and in peer groups. The "front end" causal structure of the Colvin/Pauly model is, therefore, paramount since it expresses the theory's most unique and important theoretical innovation and because the causal mechanisms it portrays provide the driving force behind subsequent causal mechanisms.

The first crucial hypothesis is that workers re-create within the family the kind of control structure they experience in the workplace. The ideal way to test this hypothesis would be to directly measure controls experienced by a sample of workers and then compare them with direct measures of the control strategies employed by those workers toward their children. For the reasons spelled out earlier, this would be extremely difficult, if not impossible. As an alternative we asked our sample of juvenile respondents to describe in detail the kind of jobs their fathers (or father surrogates) had. This information does not provide direct evidence about the actual controls experienced by the fathers, but it does permit us to classify many of the fathers into one or another of the working class Fractions described by Colvin and Pauly. According to the theorists, Fraction I workers include: "low-skilled jobs in small, nonunion manufacturing, southern textile jobs, service jobs, lower-clerical and sales jobs" (p. 532). Fraction II workers include those in the "auto, steel, and rubber industries; machine manufacture and mining," while Fraction III workers are comprised of "foremen, personal secretaries . . . wage-earning craft workers, such as electricians, carpenters, plumbers, and machinists . . . corporate and state lawyers, social workers, and school teachers" (pp. 532–33).

Following the Colvin/Pauly descriptions *exactly* (no father was classified unless the job description provided by the juvenile indicated a specific occupation that they mention in their examples) we were able to place 45 percent of the fathers into one of the three working class divisions.[5] Then using the information described earlier about the type of discipline the juvenile reported him- or herself subject to, we were able to cross-tabulate the class position of the father with the predominant method of control employed in his family. Tables 3.6 and 3.7 report the results. If Colvin and Pauly are right, Fraction I workers should mostly practice coercive control on their children, Fraction II workers should rely mainly on calculative methods, and those in Fraction III should predominantly use normative means.

But that is not what the data reveal. There is almost no relation-

TABLE 3.6
Parental Working Class vs. Type of Discipline
(Fraction of the Working Class Occupied by Parent and the Type of Discipline
Currently Used Within the Family)

| | CURRENT DISCIPLINARY TYPE | | | |
	Coercive	Calculative	Normative	Total
Fraction I	17	54	20	91
	(18.7%)	(59.3%)	(22.0%)	
Fraction II	27	85	32	144
	(18.8%)	(59.0%)	(22.0%)	
Fraction III	31	163	59	253
	(12.3%)	(64.4%)	(23.3%)	
Total	75	302	111	488
	(15.4%)	(61.9%)	(22.7%)	

Gamma = .09

TABLE 3.7
Parental Working Class vs. Type of Discipline Five Years Ago
(Fraction of the Working Class Occupied by Parent and the Type of Discipline Used
Within the Family Five Years Ago)

| | DISCIPLINARY TYPE FIVE YEARS AGO | | | |
	Coercive	Calculative	Normative	Total
Fraction I	41	42	8	91
	(45.1%)	(46.2%)	(8.8%)	
Fraction II	53	69	21	143
	(37.1%)	(48.3%)	(14.7%)	
Fraction III	91	135	25	251
	(36.3%)	(53.8%)	(10.0%)	
Total	185	246	54	485
	(38.1%)	(50.7%)	(11.1%)	

Gamma = .06

ship between the parent's location within the working class and the type of discipline used on children (gamma = .09; table 3.6) or with the type of discipline employed five years before (gamma = .06; table 3.7). Fraction I workers were as likely to use calculative means as coercive. And they were only slightly more likely to have used coercive means (45.1 percent versus 36.3 percent) and only slightly less likely to have used normative means of discipline (8.8 percent versus 10 percent, respectively) than were Fraction III workers. Overall, it appears that the most common way parents disciplined their children when they were about twelve years old was to withdraw desired privileges, *no matter what fraction of the working class they occupied.*

This is true as well for the type of discipline about age seventeen (table 3.6). Moreover, compared with five years ago, the parents were substantially less likely to use coercive techniques and more likely to use normative ones no matter what fraction of the working class they occupied. Thus the shift in disciplinary technique described earlier, away from coercive methods as the child grows older, is evident for fathers in all three fractions.

These findings challenge the Colvin/Pauly theory, for they suggest that, contrary to their "structural-Marxist" argument, experiences within different fractions of the working class are not strongly related to type of discipline likely to be used in the home. The central thesis of the theory, then, that workplace compliance structures are re-created within the family, is not supported with these data.[6]

A second argument vital to the Colvin/Pauly model states that parental control methods influence the quality of the bond between parent and child. They hypothesize specifically that coercive control methods produce negative, alienated bonds between parents and children:

> The child participates in a family control structure that contains certain rewards and punishments for specific types of behavior and perceived motives. The more coercive this structure of control, the more negative are the bonds produced in the child [p. 535].

If this hypothesis is true, we would expect to find weaker, more negative bonds between parent and child within those families where coercive techniques of discipline are employed. Our sample of approximately 1,100 students reported the nature of their relationships with each parent, along several dimensions, both currently and five years ago. Table 3.8 reports the percentage of students responding favorably to each of seven questions, classified by the type of family discipline the child indicated his or her parents used five years ago (since the results are essentially the same for

TABLE 3.8
Relationship between Nature and Strength of the Parent-Child Bond and Type of
Disciplinary Technique Employed

	Coercive Control	Calculative Control	Normative Control
"Do you feel close to your father?"			
yes	64%	69%	70%
undecided	18%	14%	13%
no	18%	17%	17%
(N)	404	555	125
"Would you like to be the kind of person your father is?"			
yes	39%	38%	36%
no	61%	62%	64%
(N)	403	554	125
"Does talking to your father help you with your problems?"			
yes	31%	33%	28%
no	69%	67%	72%
(N)	403	548	123
"Do you feel close to your mother?"			
yes	81%	81%	86%
undecided	11%	10%	6%
no	8%	9%	8%
(N)	406	556	125
"Would you like to be the kind of person your mother is?"			
yes	39%	39%	38%
no	61%	61%	62%
(N)	408	555	125
"Does talking to your mother help you with your problems?"			
yes	53%	48%	55%
no	47%	52%	45%
(N)	408	552	123
"Do you care what your parents think about you?"			
yes	86%	91%	91%
undecided	9%	5%	7%
no	5%	4%	2%
(N)	407	559	124

both points in time, only the figures for one time period are displayed).

There is clearly little difference in the quality of the affective relationship between parent and child under different punishment types. Contrary to the Colvin and Pauly argument, children who reported that their parents used coercive disciplinary methods five years ago nevertheless had as close and positive a relationship with both their parents as those who experienced normative methods of discipline. For example, 65 percent of the respondents who experienced coercive discipline reported being close to their fathers (versus 70 percent for those who had experienced normative discipline), 40 percent said they wanted to be the kinds of persons their fathers were (versus 36 percent of those who were normatively disciplined), and 31 percent (versus 28 percent of those normatively disciplined) thought that talking to their fathers helped them with their problems. There is also no difference in the strength of the relationships with the mothers. Our data suggest, then, that the quality of the parent-child bond is not contingent on the control structure in the family, but is apparently based on other factors.

Thus the two most critical links in the Colvin/Pauly theoretical model are not empirically supported in our data. There is little relationship between the objective class position of parents and the kind of discipline they impose on their children. Hence Colvin and Pauly appear to be mistaken in their contention that parents re-create the workplace compliance structure within the family. Nor does it seem to be true that a coercive compliance structure within the family is related to the strength or quality of parent-child relationships. Children who were physically and/or erratically disciplined reported just as close and positive bonds with their parents as those who were disciplined by an appeal to conscience (normative control). Hence even if the conceptual problems discussed earlier in this critique were ironed out, and even if the assumptions we discussed earlier were tenable, the theory probably would still not be very useful in providing a satisfactory explanation of "serious, patterned delinquency."

Conclusion

Although the Colvin/Pauly effort is admirable in its attempt to integrate several theoretical positions, it suffers from too many defects to be held as an exemplar. Because their formulation ignores the essential element of empirical/statistical applicability (measurement applicability and identification problems), the causal model cannot be estimated nor can straightforward hypotheses be tested unambiguously. Furthermore, conceptual ambiguities detract from the argument and make dubious assumptions necessary. Finally, empirical evidence concerning various implications of the theory suggests that its basic argument is simply incorrect. According to our data, parents' fractional location in the working class does not predict the type of child control used in the family, nor does disciplinary method predict the affective bond between child and parent. Thus in its current form, the theory appears to have quite limited value; at best it might be regarded as a "sensitizing" idea system (Blumer, 1969).

The failure of this ambitious effort at theoretical integration does not mean, of course, that a hybrid combination of the separate sets of ideas that Colvin and Pauly deal with cannot be accomplished. In fact, we think that the theory could be quite useful if it were reformulated. It is reasonable to imagine that social control in one set of a person's relationships may influence how that individual relates to others in different relationships. And it is logical to think that the social control to which one is exposed in a given set of relationships may have ultimate implications for how one behaves with respect to the law. But it is too simplistic to think that social control in the workplace represents the exclusive or even dominant influence on one's orientation toward child rearing. Moreover, if social control experienced in the family context affects the likelihood or (type) of delinquency, it seems more sensible to imagine that it does so by affecting the juvenile's moral feelings about law or his or her perception of the likelihood of being caught and punished for violation than by its effect on family, school, or peer bonds. An integrated theory that incorporates workplace control as *one of several* factors influencing child disciplinary methods, and that portrays family control structures as *one of several* factors involved in the ultimate likelihood of delinquency of various types and frequencies, would probably be more satisfactory, and constructing such a theory is certainly feasible. Therefore, the Colvin/Pauly product, although seriously flawed, should be regarded as a promising beginning.

Further, the shortcomings of the structural-Marxist theory of delinquency production should definitely not be taken as evidence that theoretical integration generally is impossible or is inappropriate. If anything, it reminds us of how essential theoretical integration actually is. Clearly, if workplace control is important to delinquency, a strictly Marxian approach will not do it justice. Similarly, a limited social-bonds theory like that set forth by Hirschi will not by itself permit us to understand who will or will not become bonded to various social groups, in what ways, or why. And the potential interconnections between social class (however conceived) and delinquency have not been fully elucidated by any extant theory (Tittle, 1983). Hence the possible linkages among social class, child rearing, social bonding, and social conformity cry out for more inclusive yet more clearly specified treatment. This more inclusive treatment will almost inevitably require theoretical integration.

The fact that Colvin and Pauly's synthesis did not succeed suggests not the futility of the enterprise, but rather the need for better integration. But those courageous enough to undertake such a task should be mindful of the problems Colvin and Pauly encountered, which all theorists encounter whether they develop original specific theories or synthesize already existing ones. In building integrated theories, as in building any kind of theory, one must stress conceptual clarity, pay close attention to empirical application, and give realistic thought to whether existing empirical evidence is consistent with the ideas as well as whether additional empirical data can be brought to bear (Freese, 1972; Gibbs, 1972; Hage, 1972). Theorists who ignore these requisites not only imperil their own work, but they may impede a healthy movement that promises a more fruitful science.

Notes

1. This is ironic because they criticize previous conceptions of social class in criminological research and theory, and attempt to replace them with an alternative "structural-Marxist" theory of class relations while at the same time according credence to the traditional measure of SES. This inconsistency probably stems from their use of the ideas of Charles Anderson (1974) in formulating their conception of class positions.

Although access to property is the major dimension of stratification in Anderson's scheme, he does note that such divisions are also distributed along dimensions of occupational income and education: "What we are arguing for is the reintroduction of property as the central variable in class analysis, assisted mainly by income analysis and secondarily by occupational analysis." Apparent adoption of this mode of thought is reflected in Colvin and Pauly's discussion of class divisions where they bring in considerations of income and education (see pp. 532–33). For example, their Fraction I workers include those in "low-skill jobs"; Fraction II workers, by comparison, are those better-educated and skilled workers who have "gained wage and benefit concessions," while Fraction III employees include scientists, technical staff, and other occupations of "higher professional and educational requirements." It is also present in their discussion of class differences in child-rearing practices, where they rely upon Kohn's (1977) research about traditional socioeconomic class position and family disciplinary practices.

2. The data collected for this analysis was part of a larger study of delinquency and drug use. The original sample of approximately 2,500 students was drawn from nine high schools in and around the city of Columbia, South Carolina. This group of 1,076 high school students represents a subsample of that group. We attached a supplement to the questionnaire that was used in the original research to which the students responded. All questionnaires were completed in small groups in the students' regular English classes, and 99 percent of those in attendance agreed to participate in the study. For additional discussion of the sample, see Paternoster and Iovanni, 1986.

3. Given the column probabilities and n size we can calculate the frequencies in each cell in table 3.5. After the eighth transition there were a total of 25 injury offenses committed by the 282 respondents [(.1084 × 166) + (.0333 × 30) + (.0377 × 53) + (.1667 × 6) + (.1111 × 27)] for a nonconditional probability of .0886.

4. Other evidence confirms these findings. Studies by Bursik (1980), Rojek and Erickson (1982), and Datesman and Aickin (1984, for status offenders) replicate Wolfgang's results indicating only a modest degree of specialization in delinquent offending. A more recent study by Farrington, Smyder, and Finnegan (1988:483), with a large sample of juvenile offenders (almost seventy thousand), twenty-one offense types, and a refined measure of specialization, also finds only weak specialization in offense patterns.

5. It is also worth noting at this point that the Colvin/Pauly theory involves an untenable assumption that only children of working-class parents

can become serious, repeat delinquents. They seem to argue that what they refer to as Fraction III workers (salaried professional, wage-earning craft workers, technical staff) and capitalists are exposed to similar work-control structures, both being characterized as "self-directing" and (presumably) disciplined by manipulated symbols and statuses. Consequently, top managers and semiautonomous wage earners, as well as the owners of the means of production, are predicted to have normative bonds to work and to reproduce normative orientations in children (p. 536) that eventually dictate conformity. But if, as their general discussion asserts, capitalists are driven by profit motives, which logically are similar to pay increases (characteristic of utilitarian control) or job security (characteristic of coercive controls) and are disciplined by market control (the competitive struggle logically producing control similar to fear of job loss or decline in pay), they could not reasonably be expected to develop normative bonds. More likely, they would have either calculative or alienated bonds and their children would be predicted to display either violent or instrumental delinquency, depending upon whether the capitalist work controls were judged to be coercive or instrumental. Nevertheless, to remain true to their own statements, we considered only those respondents whose fathers could be placed in one of the three fractions of the working class.

6. Note, however, that we are assuming that the various working class Fractions actually experience the job-related control structures that Colvin and Pauly claim. They may not, of course, but if they don't, then another crucial element of the model would be shown to be inaccurate.

References

Anderson, Charles. 1974. *The Political Economy of Social Class.* Englewood Cliffs, N.J.: Prentice-Hall.

Blumer, Herbert. 1969. *Symbolic Interactionism: Perspective and Method.* Englewood Cliffs, N.J.: Prentice-Hall.

Bohm, Robert M. 1987. "Comment on 'Traditional Contributions to Radical Criminology' by Groves and Sampson." *Journal of Research in Crime and Delinquency* 24:323–31.

Braverman, Harry. 1974. *Labor and Monopoly Capital.* New York: Monthly Review Press.

Bursik, Robert. 1980. "The Dynamics of Specialization in Juvenile Offenses." *Social Forces* 58:851–52.

Cloward, Richard, and Lloyd Ohlin. 1960. *Delinquency and Opportunity*. New York: Free Press.

Cohen, Lawrence E., and Richard Machalek. 1988. "A General Theory of Expropriative Crime: An Evolutionary Ecological Approach." *American Journal of Sociology* 94:465–501.

Colvin, Mark, and John Pauly. 1983. "A Critique of Criminology: Toward an Integrated Structural-Marxist Theory of Delinquency." *American Journal of Sociology* 89:513–51.

Conger, Rand. 1976. "Social Control and Social Learning Models of Delinquent Behavior: A Synthesis." *Criminology* 14:17–40.

Datesman, Susan, and Mikel Aickin. 1984. "Offense Specialization and Escalation among Status Offenders." *The Journal of Criminal Law and Criminology* 75:1246–75.

Edwards, Richard. 1979. *Contested Terrain: The Transformation of the Workplace in the Twentieth Century*. New York: Basic Books.

Elliott, Delbert S. 1985. "The Assumption That Theories Can Be Combined with Increased Explanatory Power: Theoretical Integration." In *Theoretical Methods in Criminology*, edited by Robert Meier, pp. 123–49. Calif.: Sage Publications.

Elliott, Delbert, Suzanne Ageton, and Rachelle Canter. 1979. "An Integrated Theoretical Perspective on Delinquent Behavior." *Journal of Research in Crime and Delinquency* 16:3–27.

Etzioni, Amitai. 1970. "Compliance Theory." In *The Sociology of Organizations*, edited by Oscar Grusky and George Miller, pp. 103–26. New York: Free Press.

Farrington, David, Howard Snyder, and Terrence Finnegan. 1988. "Specialization in Juvenile Court Careers." *Criminology* 26:461–87.

Freese, Lee. 1972. "Cumulative Sociological Knowledge." *American Sociological Review* 37:472–82.

Gibbs, Jack P. 1972. *Sociological Theory Construction*. Hinsdale, Ill.: Dryden Press.

———. 1975. *Crime, Punishment, and Deterrence*. New York: Elsevier Press.

Groves, W. Byron, and Robert J. Sampson. 1987. "Traditional Contributions to Radical Criminology." *Journal of Research in Crime and Delinquency* 24:181–214.

Hagan, John, A. R. Gillis, and John Sampson. 1985. "The Class Structure of Gender and Delinquency: Toward a Power-Control Theory of Common Delinquent Behavior." *American Journal of Sociology* 90:1,151–78.

Hage, Jerald. 1972. *Techniques and Problems of Theory Construction in Sociology*. New York: Wiley.

Hanushek, Eric A., and John E. Jackson. 1977. *Statistical Methods for Social Scientists*. New York: Academic Press.

Heise, David R. 1975. *Causal Analysis*. New York: Wiley.

Hirschi, Travis. 1969. *Causes of Delinquency*. Berkeley, Calif: University of California Press.

———. 1979. "Separate and Unequal Is Better." *Journal of Research in Crime and Delinquency* 16:34–38.

Johnson, Richard. 1979. *Juvenile Delinquency and Its Origins: An Integrated Theoretical Approach*. Cambridge: Cambridge University Press.

Kohn, Melvin. 1969. *Class and Conformity: A Study in Values*. Homewood, Ill.: Dorsey Press.

———. 1977. *Class and Conformity*. Chicago: University of Chicago Press.

Krohn, Marvin D. 1986. "The Web of Conformity: A Network Approach to the Explanation of Delinquent Behavior." *Social Problems* 33:81–93.

Liska, Allen E., Marvin Krohn, and Steven Messinger. 1989. *Theoretical Integration in Criminology*. New York: SUNY Press.

Paternoster, Raymond. 1987. "The Deterrent Effect of the Perceived Certainty and Severity of Punishment: A Review of the Evidence and Issues." *Justice Quarterly* 4:173–217.

Paternoster, Raymond, and LeeAnn Iovanni. 1986. "The Deterrent Effect of Perceived Severity: A Reexamination." *Social Forces* 64:751–77.

Rojek, Dean, and Maynard Erickson. 1982. "Reforming the Juvenile Justice System: The Diversion of Status Offenders." *Law and Society Review* 16:241.

Tittle, Charles. 1983. "Social Class and Criminal Behavior: A Critique of the Theoretical Foundation." *Social Forces* 61:334–58.

———. 1985. "The Assumption That General Theories Are Not Possible." In *Theoretical Methods in Criminology*, edited by Robert Meier, pp. 93–121. Calif.: Sage.

Wilson, James Q., and Richard J. Herrnstein. 1985. *Crime and Human Nature*. New York: Simon and Schuster.

Wolfgang, Marvin, Robert Figlio, and Thorstein Sellin. 1972. *Delinquency in a Birth Cohort*. Chicago: Chicago University Press.

Wolfgang, Marvin, Terrence Thornberry, and Robert Figlio. 1987. *From Boy to Man, from Delinquency to Crime*. Chicago: University of Chicago Press.

Wright, Eric. 1978. *Class, Crisis, and State*. London: New Left Books.

———. 1979. *Class Structure and Income Determinants*. New York: Academic Press.

4

Legal Socialization Theory: A Precursor to Comparative Research in the Soviet Union

James O. Finckenauer

Legal socialization has been defined as "the development of values, attitudes, and behaviors toward law." Legal socialization "focuses on the individual's standards for making sociolegal judgements and for resolving conflicts, pressing claims, and settling disputes" (Tapp and Levine, 1974:4). The theory of legal development is derived primarily from cognitive developmental theory. In particular, it builds upon the work of Piaget (1932) and, most especially, that of Kohlberg (1958, 1963, 1964, 1968a, 1968b, 1969). Consistent with Kohlberg's moral-development theory, legal socialization is said to progress across three stages: preconventional law obeying, conventional law maintaining, and postconventional law making (Tapp and Kohlberg, 1971; Tapp and Levine, 1974).

Individuals operating at the first (Level I) of the three stages of legal reasoning (preconventional law obeying) are guided in their reasoning by a focus on external consequences and authority. They are afraid of punishment and physical harm, and are thus particularly deferential toward power. This preconventional law deferring stance has been empirically established to be especially characteristic of younger children (Hess and Tapp, 1969; Minturn and Tapp, 1970).

Level II is a law-and-order, conformity posture. Persons operating or reasoning at this level are concerned with role expectations and their fulfillment. Most youth, by preadolescence, reason from this conventional, system-maintenance perspective. It is the predominant level of legal reasoning through adolescence and into adulthood for most adult groups (Tapp, 1987).

Postconventional (Level III) reasoning is engaged in by "[p]rincipled, thinking individuals [who] . . . see the need for social systems and yet can differentiate between the values of a given social order and universal ethics" (Tapp and Levine, 1974:22). Previous research shows relatively few persons, even among adult samples, reasoning at this level. The results of research on legal socialization are generally very similar to those produced by the moral-development research in this regard, as well as in other respects. In both instances, most persons are found to reason at the middle, conventional level, and very few people are found at the postconventional level. Just as there are age-related changes in conceptions of morality, there are age-related changes in conceptions of the law. It appears that the meaning of law loses its absolutism between childhood and adolescence, and that children become more flexible as their legal reasoning shifts from the concrete to the abstract (Radosevich and Krohn, 1981).

Cross-cultural research by Tapp and others over two decades supports the existence of a progressive legal-reasoning construct in the growth of ideas on justice and law. This research shows the following: (1) the same levels of development have occurred in all the cultures studied, (2) the pattern of legal reasoning progresses from a preconventional law deferring to a conventional law maintaining to a postconventional law making level, (3) the progression is marked by some variation showing the effects of socializing and educational experiences, and (4) these experiences can take such forms as participation in legal conflict resolution and law-related education (Tapp, 1987:4–5). A recent study by Cohn and White (1986) adds to the validity of legal developmental level as a predictor of the normative and enforcement statuses of destructive, disorderly, and social-disturbance behaviors.

The work of both cognitive development psychologists and other social scientists interested in political socialization supports the notion of age- and knowledge-related trends toward more democratic attitudes and more complex reasoning. These trends show shifts in attitudes toward wrongdoing, punishment, and the law which are progressively more liberal and humanitarian and less authoritarian (Adelson, 1971; Gallatin and Adelson, 1971; Brown, 1974; Kohlberg and Elfenbein, 1975; Mussen, Sullivan, and Eisenberg-Bergg, 1977; Wilson, 1981; Nelsen, Eisenberg, and Carroll, 1982).

Legal Knowledge

The role of legal knowledge and legal education is of particular interest here, because law-related education is a popular technique for attempting to enhance legal socialization. The position of the legal socialization theorists on legal knowledge has been stated as follows:

> We do not contend that knowledge about law determines either attitudes or behaviors. In fact, research suggests that factors such as peer influence are more important than legal knowledge. . . . In general, it is not knowledge per se but one's mode of reasoning with available information that determines the making and acting upon specific legal decisions. In our view, [however] acquiring knowledge about law (whether one endorses the law or not) is essential because information about rights, rules, expectations, and so forth expands the ability to understand problems, relate to events, and structure choices [Tapp and Levine, 1974:32].

Tapp and Levine's argument is that knowledge is a necessary, but not by itself sufficient, element in promoting progressively more sophisticated levels of legal reasoning. This knowledge must provide for understanding the basis and necessity for the rules and principles embodied in the justice system. Numerous legal or law-related education efforts have been undertaken in the United States—not always mindful of its limitations. The theoretical rationale for assuming a relationship between knowledge of the law, attitudes, and behavior has been summarized thusly:

> A common argument is that increased knowledge of the law will produce greater conformity to the law. At least three mechanisms for this effect can be suggested. One is simple reduction of error; those

who know the law are less likely to break it by mistake. . . . A second argument is that greater knowledge of the law produces greater cognitive and moral support for law; a person's behavior comes to be characterized by his intellectual convictions about the law. Both studies of moral development (e.g., Kohlberg) and social control theories of delinquency (in their inclusion of "belief in the moral validity of the law") work this vein. Finally, it may be proposed that greater knowledge of the law will produce a greater fear of the consequences of breaking it—the perceived certainty, quickness, or severity of punishment will rise with gains in knowledge, thus reducing the probability of law violation [Law-Related Education Evaluation Project, 1983:171].

The research evidence testing the link between knowledge and law-abidingness is very unpromising. The studies of legal knowledge and attitudes have found that children's knowledge of the law increases with age (Bargman, 1974; Klar, 1974; Markwood, 1975); but, attitudes toward the law seem to become increasingly negative between childhood, preadolescence, and adolescence (Portune, 1965; Klar, 1974; Markwood, 1975). This has been especially true for blacks, males, those from lower socioeconomic backgrounds, and urban youth (Bouma, 1969; Park, 1970; Torney, 1971; Liebshultz and Niemi, 1974; Fox, 1974). Jacobson and Palonsky (1981) found that greater legal knowledge did not lead to more positive attitudes toward the law, Rafky and Sealey (1975) found that legal knowledge was unrelated to either respect for the law or to disruptive behavior, and Markowitz (1986) likewise found that there was no relationship between increased knowledge of the law and improved attitudes and behavior.

On the other hand, Brown (1974) found that positive orientations toward the law, policemen, and the courts were negatively related to certain self-reported delinquency measures, Huba and Bentler (1983) found that low "law abidance" (a generalized tendency to respect the rules of law-setting institutions in society) causally preceded drug use and other deviant behaviors, and the Law-Related Education Evaluation Project (1983) found that measures of belief, for example favorable attitudes toward the police, unfavorable attitudes toward deviance, rationalizations for deviance, etc., were strongly correlated in the expected directions with self-reported delinquency.

The latter findings suggest that if young people believe in the law and the justice system, and in its equity and fairness, they may be less likely to engage in delinquency. The research does not, however, provide much support for the idea of formally, didactically educating children and youth about the law as a way of influencing their behavior.

In their study of law-related attitudes, Palonsky and Jacobson (1982) included in their sample a group of juvenile offenders confined in a state training school. They found that these offenders had more negative attitudes toward the law than did the elementary and junior high school students with whom they were compared (see Chapman, 1955–56; Portune, 1965; Fox, 1974; and Bowlus et al., 1974 for similar findings). In the comparisons between junior high students and juvenile offenders, however, the differences were not statistically significant—confirming the importance of age as a predictor of negative attitudes toward the law. Knowledge was positively, albeit modestly, correlated with attitudes. The researchers concluded that "[t]he students who know the most about the law are not necessarily those with the most favorable attitudes toward the law" (Palonsky and Jacobson, 1982:27). They also concluded that the condition of delinquency was a "moderate" predictor of negative attitudes toward the law.

Legal Socialization and Juvenile Delinquency

The Tapp/Kohlberg/Levine model of legal socialization has been criticized for a lack of interest in the behavioral consequences of legal judgements and for making the assumption that judgements are the cause of actions (Hogan and Mills, 1976). In response, Jennings, Kilkenny, and Kohlberg (1983) have argued that the relationship between moral reasoning and moral behavior is complex, but that there is a significant, though not direct relationship between them. The connection between legal reasoning and legal behavior has received less attention. Whatever the merits of these discussions, Levine concurs that past research has had mixed results in finding relationships between moral and legal reasoning processes and behavior (1979). All this is good cause to investigate the issues further—particularly with respect to the relations among knowledge of the law; belief in the moral validity, justice, and fairness of the law; other aspects of legal socialization; and juvenile delinquency.

One interesting difference in the findings from the legal-socialization and moral-development research is that the legal-socialization research that included "law deviants" as subjects did not find that those law deviants (in that particular case prison inmates) reasoned differently than college youth, teachers, or lawyers (Tapp and Levine, 1974:30). Unfortunately, this is an extremely limited finding, is not fully explainable, and, in any event, involves adult criminals as opposed to juveniles.

Some of the much more extensive moral-development research has found that juvenile delinquents do reason at a lower moral level than do nondelinquents (Fodor, 1972, 1973; Jurkovic and Prentice, 1977; Jurkovic, 1980; Sagi and Eisikovits, 1981; Jennings, Kilkenny, and Kohlberg, 1983; Hains, 1984). This has not, however, been the universal finding. Emler, Heather, and Winton (1978), for example, found that the degree and seriousness of involvement in delinquency was unrelated to immaturity of moral reasoning.

The Kohlbergians argue that lower moral reasoning is a necessary, but not sufficient cause of delinquency in that "higher reasoning makes one a more reliable moral agent and thus better able to withstand some incentives to illegal conduct" (Jennings, Kilkenny, and Kohlberg, 1983:311). Further, they say preconventional thinkers may feel less obligated to conform to any conventions—either of the larger society (in the form of society's laws) or of a subcultural group.

Although Tapp (1970) has indicated in the past that, as with moral development theory, failure to develop beyond preconventional thought between ages ten and fourteen may lead to delinquency, there is no empirical evidence to support this belief. To the contrary, in two studies, Morash (1981; 1982) found that legal reasoning was not significantly associated with seriousness of delinquency. She concluded that there was not support for "the proposition that delinquency results from failure to develop beyond a preconventional reasoning level" (Morash, 1981:367). Morash admits, however, that her studies have a number of limitations that call for further research.

Notwithstanding the many similarities between moral development and legal socialization, Levine (and Tapp and others) claims that "legal reasoning and moral judgement are not identical constructs but depict distinct, albeit related, valuation processes" (Levine, 1979:182). This, too, is good reason to investigate the relationship of "the distinct process" of legal socialization to juvenile delinquency. Does legal reasoning have any relation to delinquency? Is this relationship similar to that of moral reasoning? If not, how and why is it different?

A related theoretical construct that also argues for further research comes from the work of sociologist Travis Hirschi (1969). It is this construct that helps explain the findings about belief mentioned earlier. Hirschi's social control theory is very compatible with moral development and legal socialization theories. In fact, Kohlberg and his colleagues have indicated that "[t]he portion of delinquent behavior that is explained by immature moral reasoning is most theoretically and empirically compatible with social-control theory" (Jennings, Kilkenny, and Kohlberg, 1983:347). One of the key components of social control theory is the principle of "belief in the moral validity of social rules." It offers the proposition that there is variation in the extent to which people—including children and young people—believe they should obey the rules of society, and that the less a person believes he should obey the rules, the more likely he is to violate them (Hirschi, 1969:26).

In his test of this thesis, Hirschi found that there was variation in the extent to which the boys in his study believed they should obey the law; and, the less they believed they should obey it, the less likely they were to do so. Respect for the law was strongly related to the commission of delinquent acts. As concern for the morality of delinquent acts declined, the greater was the likelihood that they would be committed (Hirschi, 1969:204–5).

Building on this foundation, it might be that to the extent that legal socialization involves young people internalizing the normative rules, social conventions, and moral codes of their society, to that extent the level of their legal socialization will be related to their likelihood of rule breaking, convention breaking, code breaking, and law breaking, that is, juvenile delinquency.

Cross-Cultural, Comparative Studies

The principal cross-cultural, comparative study of legal socialization was conducted in 1965 (Hess and Tapp, 1969). In that study,

406 preadolescent (ages ten to fourteen) children from six countries were interviewed. In addition to the United States, the countries represented in the sample were Denmark, Greece, India, Italy, and Japan. That research collected information on children's perceptions of and attitudes toward authority, rules, and aggression in various compliance systems such as the home, school, government, and community. This research demonstrated that there was universality in the modes of legal reasoning, and that there were cross-cultural commonalities among the preadolescents in the six countries and seven cultures (both black and white samples were employed in the United States) (Tapp and Levine, 1974).

There are a number of characteristics and factors concerning this research which make new cross-cultural studies imperative. First is the concern that the results may be dated, and that the conclusions therefore may no longer be valid. Have there been relevant historical effects over the last twenty-five years that would influence these findings?

Second, the countries from which the samples were taken included only a limited number of Western-style democracies. Would children and youth from other countries with other cultural and legal traditions respond differently? In particular, would young people in the Soviet Union, Saudi Arabia, or Nigeria, for example, experience their legal worlds and construct their maps of legality differently?

Third, methodologically, the original open-ended interview format used in the 1960s has been revised and reduced to a shorter, forced-choice questionnaire format. Although the latter form has produced reliable and valid results in the United States, it has not yet been utilized in cross-cultural research.

Fourth, the information collected in the cross-cultural studies did not include information on knowledge of the law, on attitudes toward the law and the justice system, on beliefs in the justice and fairness of the legal system, nor on behavior. In particular, it did not encompass delinquency as a variable. As was pointed out earlier, this has been true of all legal socialization research to date; that is, the relation between legal socialization and juvenile delinquency has not been examined.

Legal Socialization in the U.S.S.R.

There have been no studies in the Soviet Union of the Tapp/ Kohlberg/Levine theory of legal socialization. There have, however, been cross-cultural studies of socialization (for example, Bronfenbrenner, 1970; Whyte, 1977), of political socialization in the U.S.S.R. (for example, Clawson, 1973; Berman, 1977), of moral judgement (for example, Ziv, Shani, and Nebenhaus, 1975), and of legal education (for example, Ioffe, 1978; Gerbich, 1978; Sukharev, 1978; Fomin, 1978). Other Soviet scholars have also considered the issues of public consciousness as it relates to crime and punishment (for example, Yakovlev, 1987; Kogan, 1987) and the internalization of legal norms and values (for example, Lukasheva, 1987).

The principal conclusions and implications of this literature— which lays the foundations for new research initiatives—are as follows:

- The Soviet collective-centered system of child rearing, with its emphasis upon character education, should produce children who are more conforming, and less anti-adult, rebellious, aggressive, and delinquent than American children (Bronfenbrenner, 1970; Whyte, 1977). With advancing modernization, however, has come—and will continue to come—increasing juvenile delinquency, hooliganism, and other kinds of antisocial behavior (Clawson, 1973). How do American and Soviet children of the late-twentieth-century variety compare on these dimensions?
- Cultural socialization processes in the U.S.S.R. have a strong influence on moral judgement (Ziv, Shani, and Nebenhaus, 1978). One of the results of these processes is that, although Kohlbergian developmental sequences may appear in Soviet society, the passage to higher levels could be expected to be slower. If so, is this true of legal socialization as well?
- Formal legal instruction in the schools is intended to shape the civic views of young people, and to develop in them a sense of personal responsibility, convince them of the inevitability of punishment for crime, and to prevent legal infractions. Such instruction was deemed necessary when surveys indicated that Soviet students were almost completely ignorant of the law. It is believed that "[k]nowledge and understanding of the law strongly

influence young people's behavior'' (Ioffe, 1978:38) and that organized legal education will reduce criminality and other anti-social behavior among young people (Sukharev, 1978). How do American and Soviet children and youth compare in their legal knowledge? Are the relations among knowledge, attitudes, and behavior different in the Soviet Union than they have been in the United States?

• Both Soviet and outside observers have noted a malaise among Soviet youth, and a possibly consequential rise in juvenile crime, drug use, and other deviant behavior (Keller, 1987; Finckenauer, 1988). Is this the case? How does the situation compare with that in the United States?

Conclusions

A number of other important theoretical questions—in addition to those mentioned above—can be raised, which would make comparative research with the Soviet Union imperative in this area. The same, of course, would be true of other countries as well. It is not an overstatement to conclude that this is all virtually unexplored territory.

In one respect this is a very curious phenomenon. It is unfortunately the case that in too many areas of social science in general, and in criminology in particular, there is much empirical work that is either atheoretical or at least has little benefit from sound theorizing. There is a considerable amount of quantitative rehashing of the old, tried-and-true theories of crime and delinquency. It is this rather low state of the art that is the principal raison d'être for the serial *Advances in Criminological Theory*.

In the case of legal socialization theory, the reverse is true. There is a fair amount of theorizing, but relatively little empirical work. This is particularly so in terms of cross-cultural, comparative research examining the links between legal socialization and behavior. Here there seems to be an opportunity to truly make some advances in criminological theory.

References

Adelson, J. 1971. "The Political Imagination of the Young Adolescent." *Daedalus*, Fall:1013–49.

Bargman, G. F. 1974. *A Study of Knowledge and Attitudes toward the Bill of Rights in Selected Iowa School Districts.* Ph.D. dissertation, University of Iowa.

Berman, Harold J. 1977. "The Use of Law to Guide People to Virtue: A Comparison of Soviet and U.S. Perspectives." In *Law, Justice and The Individual in Society,* edited by J. L. Tapp and F. J. Levine. New York: Holt, Rinehart, and Winston.

Bouma, Donald. 1969. *Kids and Cops: A Study in Mutual Hostility.* Grand Rapids, Mich.: William B. Erdman.

Bowlus, D. et al. 1974. *A Study of Youth Attitudes toward Authority and Their Relationship to School Adjustment Patterns.* ERIC Document Reproduction Service, no. ED 096 088.

Bronfenbrenner, Urie. 1970. *Two Worlds of Childhood.* New York: Russell Sage Foundation.

Brown, Don W. 1974. "Cognitive Development and Willingness to Comply with Law." *American Journal of Political Science* 18(3):583–94.

Chapman, A. 1955–56. "Attitudes toward Legal Authorities of Juveniles: A Comparative Study of Delinquents and Non-Delinquent Boys." *Sociology and Social Research* 40:170–75.

Clawson, Robert W. 1973. "Political Socialization of Children in the USSR." *Political Science Quarterly* 27:187–203.

Cohn, Ellen S., and Susan O. White. 1986. "Cognitive Development versus Social Learning Approaches to Studying Legal Socialization." *Basic and Applied Social Psychology* 7:195–209.

Emler, Nicholas P., Nick Heather, and Maurice Winton. 1978. "Delinquency and the Development of Moral Reasoning." *British Journal of Clinical Psychology* 17:325–31.

Finckenauer, James O. 1988. "Juvenile Delinquency in the USSR: Social Structural Explanations." *International Journal of Comparative and Applied Criminal Justice* 12(1):73–80.

Fodor, Eugene M. 1972. "Delinquency and Susceptibility to Social Influence among Adolescents as a Function of Level of Moral Development." *The Journal of Social Psychology* 86:257–60.

Fodor, Eugene M. 1973. "Moral Development and Parent Behavior Antecedents in Adolescent Psychopaths." *The Journal of Genetic Psychology* 122:37–43.

Fomin, N. S. 1978. "Factors in Legalistic Education and the Methods Used to Determine the Results of Their Influence." *Soviet Education* August:46–59.

Fox, K. A. 1974. *Law and Justice: Adolescents' Perceptions of Policemen.* ERIC Document Reproduction Service, no. ED 095 033.

Fraser, Barry J., and David L. Smith. 1980. "Assessment of Law-Related Attitudes." *Social Education* May:406–9.

Gallatin, J., and J. Adelson. 1971. "Legal Guarantees of Individual Freedom: A Cross-National Study of the Development of Political Thought. In *Law, Justice, and the Individual in Society,* edited by J. L. Tapp and F. J. Levine. New York: Holt, Rinehart, and Winston.

Gerbich, A. I. 1978. "Experience Gained in the Legalistic Education of School Pupils." *Soviet Education,* August:60–69.

Hains, Anthony A. 1984. "Variables in Social Cognitive Development: Moral Judgment, Role-Taking, Cognitive Processes, and Self-Concept in Delinquents and Nondelinquents." *Journal of Early Adolescence* 4(1):65–74.

Hess, R. D., and J. L. Tapp. 1969. *Authority, Rules, and Aggression: A Cross-National Study of the Socialization of Children into Compliance Systems.* Part 1. Washington, D.C.: United States Department of Health, Education, and Welfare.

Hirschi, T. 1969. *Causes of Delinquency.* Berkeley, Calif.: University of California Press.

Hogan, Robert, and Carol Mills. 1976. "Legal Socialization." *Human Development* 19:261–76.

Hraba, Joseph, Martin G. Miller, and Vincent J. Webb. 1975. "Mutability and Delinquency: The Relative Effects of Structural, Associational, and Attitudinal Variables on Juvenile Delinquency." *Criminal Justice and Behavior* 2(4):408–20.

Huba, G. J., and P. M. Bentler. 1983. "Causal Models of the Development of Law Abidance and Its Relationship to Psycho-Social Factors and Drug Use." In *Personality Theory, Moral Development, and Criminal Behavior,* edited by William S. Laufer and James M. Day. Lexington, Mass.: Heath.

Ioffe, M. G. 1978. "Nurturing Respect for the Law." *Soviet Education* August:37–45.

Irving, Kym, and Michael Siegal. 1983. "Mitigating Circumstances in Children's Perceptions of Criminal Justice: The Case of an Inability to Control Events." *British Journal of Developmental Psychology* 1:179–88.

Jacobson, Michael G., and Stuart B. Palonsky. 1981. "Effects of Law-Related Education Program." *The Elementary School Journal* 82:49–57.

Jennings, William S., Robert Kilkenny, and Lawrence Kohlberg. 1983. "Moral-Development Theory and Practice for Youthful Offenders." In *Personality Theory, Moral Development, and Criminal Behavior,* edited by William S. Laufer and James M. Day. Lexington, Mass.: Heath.

Jurkovic, Gregory J., and Norman M. Prentice. 1977. "Relation of Moral and Cognitive Dimensions of Juvenile Delinquency." *Journal of Abnormal Psychology* 86(4):414–20.

Jurkovic, Gregory J. 1980. "The Juvenile Delinquent as a Moral Philosopher: A Structural-Developmental Perspective." *Psychological Bulletin* 88(3):709–27.

Keller, Bill. 1987. "Russia's Restless Youth." *The New York Times Magazine*, 26 July:14–53.

Klar, W. H. 1974. *An Inquiry into the Knowledge of an Attitude Toward the Law on the Part of Public School Students in Connecticut.* Ph.D. dissertation, University of Connecticut.

Kohlberg, L. 1958. *The Development of Modes of Moral Thinking and Choice in the Years Ten to Sixteen.* Ph.D. dissertation, University of Chicago.

——. 1963. "The Development of Children's Orientations toward a Moral Order. I. Sequence of Moral Thought." *Vita Humana* 6:11–33.

——. 1964. "Development of Moral Character and Moral Ideology." In *Review of Child Development Research*, vol. 1, edited by M. I. Hoffman. New York: Russell Sage Foundation.

——. 1968a. "The Child as a Moral Philosopher." *Psychology Today* 2(4):24–31.

——. 1968b. "Moral Development." In *International Encyclopedia of the Social Sciences*. New York: Macmillan.

——. 1969. "Stage and Sequence: The Cognitive-Developmental Approach to Socialization." In *Handbook of Socialization Theory and Research*, edited by D. A. Goslin. Chicago: Rand McNally.

Kohlberg, L., and D. Elfenbein. 1975. "The Development of Moral Judgement Concerning Capital Punishment." *American Journal of Orthopsychiatry* 45:614–40.

Kogan, Victor M. 1987. "Punishment under Criminal Law and the Public Consciousness." Unpublished abstract presented at Rutgers, translated by Stephen P. Dunn and Ethel Dunn.

Lapsley, Daniel K., Michael R. Harwell, Leanne M. Olson, Daniel Flannery, and Stephen M. Quintana. 1984. "Moral Judgement, Personality, and Attitude to Authority in Early and Late Adolescence." *Journal of Youth and Adolescence* 13(6):527–42.

Law-Related Education Evaluation Project. 1983. *Social Science Education Consortium.* Boulder, Colo.: Center for Action Research.

Levine, F. J. 1979. *The Legal Reasoning of Youth: Dimensions and Correlates.* Ph.D. dissertation, University of Chicago.

Liebshultz, S. F., and R. C. Niemi. 1974. "Political Attitudes among Black Children." In *The Politics of Future Citizens*, edited by R. C. Niemi. San Francisco: Jossey-Bass Inc.

Lukasheva, E. A. 1987. "The Social-Psychological Mechanism of Internalization of Legal Norms and Values by the Individual." Unpublished abstract presented at Rutgers, translated by Stephen P. Dunn and Ethel Dunn.

Markwood, J. M. 1975. *Knowledge and Attitudes Regarding the Juvenile Justice System among Delinquent and Non-Delinquent Youth.* Ph.D. dissertation, University of Virginia.

Markowitz, Alan. 1986. ''The Impact of Law Related Education on Elementary Children in Reducing Deviant Behavior.'' Ph.D. dissertation, Rutgers University.

Minturn, L., and J. L. Tapp. 1970. *Authority, Rules, and Aggression: A Cross-National Study of Children's Judgments of the Justice of Aggressive Confrontations.* Part 2. Washington, D.C.: United States Department of Health, Education, and Welfare.

Morash, Merry Ann. 1981. ''Cognitive Developmental Theory: A Basis for Juvenile Correctional Reform?'' *Criminology* 19(3):360–71.

———. 1982. ''Relationships of Legal Reasoning to Social Class, Closeness to Parents, and Exposure to a High Level of Reasoning among Adolescents Varying in Seriousness of Delinquency.'' *Psychology Reports* 50:755–60.

Mussen, P., L. Sullivan, and N. Eisenberg-Berg. 1977. ''Changes in Political-Economic Attitudes during Adolescence.'' *Journal of Genetic Psychology* 130:69–76.

Nelsen, Edward A., Nancy Eisenberg, and James L. Carroll. 1982. ''The Structure of Adolescents' Attitudes toward Law and Crime.'' *The Journal of Genetic Psychology* 140:47–58.

Niles, William Jeremiah. 1983. *The Effects of Moral Education on Delinquents and Predelinquents.* Ph.D. dissertation, Fordham University.

———. 1986. ''Effects of a Moral Development Discussion Group on Delinquent and Predelinquent Boys.'' *Journal of Counseling Psychology* 33(1):45–51.

Palonsky, Stuart B., and Michael G. Jacobson. 1982. ''The Measurement of Law-Related Attitudes.'' *Journal of Social Studies Research* 6(1):22–28.

Park, J. C. 1970. *Chicago Suburban and Inner-City Student Opinion and Achievement Related to Law in American Society.* Ph.D. dissertation, Northwestern University.

Piaget, J. 1932. *The Moral Judgment of the Child.* New York: Kegan, Paul, Trench, Trubner.

Portune, R. G. 1965. *An Analysis of Attitudes of Junior High School Pupils toward Police Officers Applied to the Preparation of a Work of Juvenile Fiction.* Ph.D. dissertation, University of Cincinnati.

Prepodavanie istori v sredneishkde, Editors of. 1978. ''On Improving the Organization of Instruction in the Course 'Fundamental Principles of the Soviet State and Law' in the Eighth Grade of General Education Schools." *Soviet Education* August: 70–81.

Radosevich, Marcia J., and Marvin Krohn. 1981. "Cognitive Moral Development and Legal Socialization." *Criminal Justice and Behavior* 8(4):401–24.

Rafky, David M., and Ronald W. Sealey. 1975. "The Adolescent and the Law: A Survey." *Crime and Delinquency* 21:131–38.

Sagi, Abraham, and Zvi Eisikovits. 1981. "Juvenile Delinquency and Moral Development." *Criminal Justice and Behavior* 8(1).

Saltzstein, Herbert, and Sharon Osgood. 1975. "The Development of Children's Reasoning about Group Interdependence and Obligation." *The Journal of Psychology* 90:147–55.

Siegal, Michael. 1984. "Diminished Responsibility as a Mitigating Circumstance in Juvenile Offenders' Legal Judgments." *Journal of Adolescence* 7:233–43.

Sukharev, A. 1978. "The Legalistic Education of the Younger Generation." *Soviet Education* August:6–21.

Tapp, June L. 1970. "A Child's Garden of Law and Order." *Psychology Today* December.

———. 1987. "The Jury as a Socializing Experience: A Socio-Cognitive View." In *Advances in Forensic Psychology and Psychiatry,* vol. 2, edited by Robert W. Rieber. Norwood, N.J.: Ablex Publishing Corp.

Tapp, June L., and Felice Levine. 1974. "Legal Socialization: Strategies for an Ethical Legality." Reprinted from *Stanford Law Review* 27(1), by the Board of Trustees of the Leland Stanford Junior University.

Tapp, June L., and Lawrence Kohlberg. 1971. "Developing Senses of Law and Legal Justice." *Journal of Social Issues* 27(2):65–91.

Torney, J. V. 1977. "Socialization of Attitudes toward the Legal System." In *Law, Justice and the Individual in Society,* edited by J. L. Tapp and F. L. Levine. New York: Holt, Rinehart, and Winston.

Yakovlev, A. M. 1987. "Criminalization and Stereotypes of Public Consciousness." Unpublished abstract presented at Rutgers, translated by Stephen P. Dunn and Ethel Dunn.

Wall, Shavaun, and Mary Furlong. 1985. "Comprehension of Miranda Rights by Urban Adolescents with Law-Related Education." *Psychological Reports* 56:359–72.

Whyte, Martin King. 1977. "Child Socialization in the Soviet Union and China." *Studies in Comparative Communism* 10(3):235–59.

Wilson, Richard W. 1981. "Political Socialization and Moral Development." *World Politics* 33(3):153–77.

Ziv, Avener, Abraham Shani, and Shoshana Nebenhaus. 1975. "Adolescents Educated in Israel and in the Soviet Union: Differences in Moral Judgment." *Journal of Cross-Cultural Psychology* 6(1).

5

Theoretical Explanations of Race Differences in Heroin Use

Jeanette Covington

Heroin addicts are under obvious pressures to commit crimes to support their habits. Yet there is some variation in crime rates within addict populations. In general, efforts to explain such variations in crime rates have been concerned with conditions where community, school, or family controls may be weakened, as with social bond or social disorganization theories (Kornhauser, 1978; Hirschi, 1969; Shaw and McKay, 1972; Bursik and Webb, 1982). Crime has also been understood in terms of reinforcements from deviant peers or as an outgrowth of neutralizations employed by offenders to excuse or justify their acts. For offenders who persist in crime into their adult years, their degree of commitment to conventional institutions is also seen as important in understanding why they continue deviant careers or why their criminal activities are gradually reduced.

In this study, an effort is made to determine how crucial these explanations are in accounting for levels of criminality among young-adult heroin users. Further, because it is expected that the conditions surrounding the initiation and maintenance of drug life-styles may differ by race, the impact of these theories on levels of criminality are considered separately for blacks and whites.

In the first section, the literature on each of these theories is reviewed with an eye to identifying expected racial differences in their impact on crime. The following two sections are concerned with a description of the sample and an explanation of how dependent and independent variables were measured. The results are briefly discussed in the section which follows, and these findings are then summarized and discussed.

Literature Review

The theories to be tested in this study—social disorganization/ social bond, differential association/social learning, neutralization, and commitment to conventional institutions—will be briefly reviewed in the first part of this section and then expected race differences in the impact of these theories on criminality will be discussed.

Social Disorganization Theory

Social disorganization theorists assume that motivation to commit crime is constant, that everyone would commit crime if given a chance. What varies for them is the exercise of informal controls. Hence crime tends to be high in those communities and those families where informal controls have been undermined. They argue that informal controls were strong in rural America and European peasant communities and were undermined with the rural and European migration to large American cities. In part, these controls were weakened because American urban communities were ethnically heterogeneous; hence no single local culture or historical tradition existed to draw neighbors together. In light of this, individuals were no longer concerned with the opinions of their neighbors, and informal controls such as gossip and ostracism—which traditionally had force—were no longer sufficient to keep them from flaunting community standards (Homans, 1950; Faris, 1948; Shaw and McKay, 1972).

Informal controls were also weakened due to the high rates of residential mobility that characterized urban communities. Mobility was high because a stream of immigrants was constantly moving into these neighborhoods upon their arrival in the city. Further, others were constantly moving out as they made enough money to be able to afford housing in more affluent areas. Anonymity flourished under these conditions of high mobility and as a result, the ostracism and the gossip that had controlled crime in the small rural and peasant communities were not effective because persons were no longer concerned with what little-known neighbors thought of them.

Finally, because disorganization was associated with the areas of first settlement of the immigrant poor, an inverse relationship between class and crime was assumed. Indeed because these were areas of first settlement, these communities of newcomers were presumed to be the most inexperienced and therefore the least equipped to grapple with the heterogeneity and mobility of these urban neighborhoods.

Weakened community controls meant that area juveniles were free to engage in various acts of delinquency without fear that adult neighbors would report to their parents. Parents were often unknown to the neighbors, particularly when families moved around a lot. This adversely affected the families of these juveniles as parental supervision of children was no longer supplemented by neighbors. Hence, community disorganization exacerbated family disorganization.

Social Bond Theories

These early social disorganization theories have subsequently been criticized. In particular, the theorists themselves have been described as rural moralists who saw the city in negative terms and saw urbanization as a disorganizing force (Kornhauser, 1978; Clinard, 1968). It is argued that urbanization might have better been seen in more neutral terms as social change rather than disorganization. This approach allows for the eventual adjustment of urban residents to the heterogeneity and mobility of the city several decades later.

Hence, social bond theorists have begun with some of the same assumptions but have approached the problem in slightly different fashion. Much like the social disorganization theorists, social bond theorists assume that everyone would deviate if given a chance. They too argue that it is informal controls that prevent deviation, but they are more concerned with understanding the process by which an individual's bonds to conventional society are broken

(Hirschi, 1969; Kornhauser, 1978). Hence, they concentrate on the individual's detachment from the family, the school, and peers rather than examining those environments that undermine informal controls.

They argue that juveniles who are strongly attached to their families avoid crime because they are concerned about their families' favorable opinions of them (Hirschi, 1969). Other juveniles, who are committed to long-range goals such as continuing their education and getting a good job, are also concerned about what teachers think of them. Hence they work hard in school and attempt to gain their teachers' respect. Because of their attachments to family and school, juveniles have a stake in conformity and hence avoid crime. By contrast, juveniles who lack such attachments have no stake in conformity and are free to deviate.

Social Learning and Differential Association Theories

Unlike the social bond theorists, the social learning and differential association theorists allow for the possibility that deviance may be socially rewarding (Sutherland and Cressey, 1955; Akers, 1977; Akers et al., 1979; Elliott, Huizinga, and Ageton, 1985). Individuals turn to deviance because they are reinforced by deviant peers rather than merely because they are detached from conventional society. The approval of deviant friends may then provide sufficient rewards for juveniles to overcome the disapproval of conventional society. In explaining how deviants reconcile their behavior to conventional standards, it is suggested that deviant groups may override the moral evaluations of conventional society without reversing them. In part, conventional standards may be overridden because of the juvenile's more frequent contacts with deviant groups (Sutherland and Cressey, 1955). However, these frequent contacts need not result in socialization to explicitly deviant values. Rather, frequent contacts with deviants may mean that individuals come to see deviant behavior as the norm in a statistical sense. In other words, they may overestimate the amount of deviance committed by others and thus see their own behavior as little different from that of other juveniles (Elliott, Huizinga, and Ageton, 1985). Juveniles may also see their friends as more approving of deviance than they are themselves and may find themselves modeling their behavior after their deviant friends in an effort to identify with them and receive social reinforcements.

Neutralization Theory

In seeking to override conventional moral evaluations of deviant behavior, individuals may also resort to neutralizations. That is, they may seek to excuse or justify their behavior by suggesting that they are not morally responsible for their behavior or by condemning those who would condemn them (Sykes and Matza, 1957; Minor, 1981). In so doing, they do not really question the rightness of conventional morality; rather, they introduce extenuating circumstances that suggest that these standards do not apply to their behavior.

Commitment to Conventional Institutions

The theories discussed thus far tend to emphasize what causes individuals to initiate crime and hence focus on juveniles beginning their deviant careers. As such, they may not be sufficient to explain criminality in the sample of young-adult heroin users discussed in this study. Therefore the effects of adult *commitment to conventional institutions* will also be considered.

Generally, this literature emphasizes the degree to which the adult criminal has a stake in conformity to conventional institutions. When commitment to conventional institutions is examined in these studies, there is a tendency to stress the importance of religious, educational, and work-related institutions (Ginsberg and Greeley, 1978; Knox, 1981; Holzman, 1982). The relationship between crime and work-related institutions has received particular attention largely because an antagonistic relationship is presumed to exist between work and crime (Berk, Lenihan, and Rossi, 1980; Holzman, 1982; Thornberry and Farnsworth, 1982). For one thing, holding a legitimate job leaves less time for competing criminal involvements. Further, employment is associated with valued statuses and higher self-esteem within deviant populations (Liker, 1982; Covington, 1986). Indeed, the fear of losing income or security is thought to explain lower crime rates among employed ex-felons, who see an arrest as a threat to their livelihood. Hence, employment encourages commitment to conventional lifestyles.

In these studies, it is also assumed that a socialization process occurs in which nondeviant coworkers encourage the criminal to assimilate conventional values. The fact that labor-force participation is correlated with other measures of social integration—such as being married and having children—supports the notion that low crime rates can be explained by differential exposure to conventional values (Berk, Lenihan, and Rossi, 1980; Knox, 1981; Akers et al., 1979). In fact, it is argued that some felons may 'quit' crime and seek out employment to regain respectability and maintain familial ties (Sviridoff and Thompson, 1983).

However, some research questions the presumed antagonistic relationship between work and crime (Luckenbill and Best, 1981; Best and Luckenbill, 1982; Liker, 1982). It is argued that for many less-professional criminals, both crime and legal work may be low paying. Offenders may supplement insufficient proceeds from crime with wages earned from legal employment.

Expected Race Differences

It could be argued that certain of these theories might better account for levels of criminality among blacks than whites, and that the routes by which these groups come to initiate drug and criminal life-styles may differ. For example, social disorganization theories may have particular relevance for blacks at the onset of their deviant careers since they are more likely to live in urban areas characterized by mobility and heterogeneity—conditions associated with 'disorganization' by early theorists (Shaw and McKay, 1972). Further, blacks have been described as relatively recent migrants to the city so that they most closely resemble the European immigrants of the early twentieth century (Spergel, 1984; Yablonsky, 1970). However, there is a problem with applying social disorganization theory in this fashion because it tends to focus on conditions that characterize a community while ignoring *extracommunity* factors that may cause disorganization and thus influence neighborhood crime rates.

Indeed with black communities, extracommunity factors may be especially crucial. For one thing, it is argued that police have traditionally contained crime within these areas, so many criminal organizations have willingly located there. This has been especially true for the marketers of heroin, as the heroin trade in particular has flourished in these areas since World War II (Staff of NEWSDAY, 1974; Chein et al., 1964; Ball, 1970). Secondly, many black communities emerged under conditions of extreme mobility for, as blacks integrated some neighborhoods, whites rapidly moved out. The very speed with which population turnover occurred in these instances meant that the emerging communities were deprived of preestablished community organizations; they were left ill-equipped to grapple with crime (Bursik and Webb, 1982). Such communities would have been quite vulnerable to invasion by criminal populations, according to social disorganization theory, as they could do little to fend off crime. In addition, relations between the police and the community tend to be poor in black areas, and levels of resident distrust of the police are high (Hahn, 1971; Hagan and Albonetti, 1982; Jacob, 1971; Spear, 1968). A long tradition of residential segregation has also meant that many stable working-class or low-income families coexist with unemployed, unattached, unmarried males (Hannerz, 1969; Liebow, 1967). Since many of these males lack a stake in the community they may be likely to turn to crime. Hence, they may well provide a ready pool of offenders who can train neighborhood juveniles in the necessary criminal skills.

This suggests that black juveniles may have especially easy access to criminal opportunities and that exposure to criminal populations may cut across a wider range of class levels among blacks than whites.

These ecological conditions not only undermine the community's social controls, but they may also affect the juvenile's social bonds to family and school. In other words, families and local schools may experience difficulties in supervising juveniles in communities where criminal opportunities abound. Indeed, Hannerz (1969) notes that many parents complain about these conditions and attempt to protect their children by prohibiting them from frequenting certain street corners, alleys, pool halls, and barber shops. Family and school supervision may be especially crucial, as any interruption of parental or school surveillance may result in juvenile exposure to deviant life-styles. Indeed, these juveniles may require an almost excessive degree of parental and school control. Detachment from family and school in neighborhoods where drugs and crime are endemic may then have enormous impact on early involvement with deviance and heroin. Because black users are more likely to hail from areas with criminal traditions, it is expected that evidence of detachment from family and school may have particular application to them.

A number of white users also initiated their careers in urban areas where drug use was endemic (Hughes and Crawford, 1974); however with the drug epidemic of the late 1960s, substance use spread to suburban neighborhoods where street cultures were not entrenched. It seems likely that community and family controls would be less crucial under these conditions as unsupervised youth would not have such ready access to criminal traditions. Indeed, suburban users were often either isolated or in contact with only a few other experimenters in their neighborhoods (Hughes and Crawford, 1974). Those who wished to progress beyond occasional experimentation were virtually required to associate with like-minded individuals.

Experimentation with a variety of drugs was in fact becoming increasingly widespread among whites in the early 1970s, and it peaked by the end of the 1970s (Johnston, O'Malley, and Bachman, 1986). Hence, it was possible that many of these users saw their behavior as little different from other juveniles and may have been inclined to model themselves after drug-using friends and to seek out the social reinforcements that came with widespread drug experimentation.

Once addicted, enormous pressures were placed on these users to turn to illegal means to support an increasingly costly habit (Covington, 1979). Generally, then, criminality was associated with a process of increased detachment from conventional associates and greater attachment to other heroin users. Such differential association with other addicts allowed for the early apprenticeship and involvement of these users in criminal acts for the support of the habit. Association with deviant others may, then, be of central importance for suburban users and thus *differential association* and *social learning* predictors would be expected to have greater impact on offense levels among whites.

Racial differences are also expected with *neutralization theory,* with these predictors better accounting for variations in black crime rates. Specifically, black addicts are expected to be more inclined to condemn their condemners (police, court system) than whites and hence such accounts should have more force in encouraging criminality. The tendency to condemn the criminal justice system is actually quite widespread among blacks—deviant and nondeviant—who often regard the police and the courts as less fair in their administration of justice than do whites (Hahn, 1971; Jacob, 1971; Hagan and Albonetti, 1982). Distrust of the criminal justice system is likely to be even more pronounced among deviant blacks—such as heroin users—who may regard their treatment at the hands of legal authorities as particularly severe and who may be more inclined toward such perceptions than white users (Covington, 1987). Because black users might be likely to see the system as less fair than whites, they might more readily resort to neutralizations as a means of justifying and persisting in criminal behavior. Hence, neutralization would be more highly correlated with criminality among blacks.

Finally, no racial differences are expected in the impact of *commitment to conventional institutions* on criminality. In particular, employment may not have much impact on offense levels for either group. While blacks generally report higher unemployment levels and less stable employment than whites (Wilson, 1978; Diprete, 1981; Calvin, 1981), there may be some tendency to combine legal employment and crime in both groups. This may be especially true in a sample of heroin addicts who are notably unprofessional at crime. Hence, the presumed antagonistic relationship between work and crime would not hold.

Sample and Data

This research is based on data drawn from a larger study funded by the National Institute on Drug Abuse. Personal interviews were conducted with 204 black addicts and 168 white addicts entering publicly funded treatment programs in Miami, Los Angeles, and Detroit in 1975–76. Treatment programs were selected for the study if they were accepting new clients during the data-collection period. All new admittees were asked to participate although their eligibility for treatment was not affected if they refused. The interviews lasted two-and-a-half hours on the average and respondents were paid $4.50 an hour upon completion of the interview. The interviewers were trained nonstudents and conducted interviews with clients within three weeks after admission. This minimized the effect of treatment status.

In addition to the data drawn from the study questionnaires, data were also taken from admissions forms. These forms were filled out by program staff for *all* persons admitted to treatment. They provided information on criminal histories and background characteristics. The appropriate admissions forms were then matched with the study questionnaires for the 372 respondents in the sample.

The majority of these respondents were enrolled in two types of treatment programs—methadone maintenance (54.3 percent) and drug-free therapeutic communities (42.2 percent). While enrollment in these programs suggests a commitment to eventual rehabilitation, many of these respondents had not entered these programs voluntarily. Only 34.2 percent of the methadone admittees and 16.8 percent of the therapeutic-community clients could be classified as voluntary admissions. Even these figures may be inflated, as many of these self-referrals enter treatment for a temporary respite from drugs rather than rehabilitation. Also, many program clients maintain an ongoing relationship with street subcultures and persist in drug use while enrolled in these programs.

The sample was split almost evenly by race: 54.9 percent of the respondents were black and 45.1 percent were white. Female users were over-sampled, resulting in a population which was 45.6 percent female and 54.4 percent male. For the most part, the respondents were young adults and there were no racial differences in age: the mean age for blacks was 26.9 years and for whites, 26.2 years. There were also similarities in terms of initial drug use: 65.5 percent of the black users and 59.2 percent of the whites began experimentation with illegal drugs by using marijuana. Heroin and other opiates were the second most popular initial drugs for blacks (17.8 percent), while barbituates (11.9 percent) and amphetamines (11.9 percent) were ranked after heroin for white users. White users initiated illegal drug use at a significantly younger age (mean = 13.95 years) than blacks (mean = 16.41 years), and for both groups, roughly three years elapsed in their progression to heroin. Hence, whites began using heroin at a mean age of 17.56 years while blacks reported a mean onset age of 19.33 years. Due to their earlier initiation to heroin, white respondents reported slightly longer drug careers than blacks; they had used an average of 8.64 years compared to 7.64 years for blacks.

Many of these users hail from low-income backgrounds, although this is more marked among black respondents. Blacks report that both their mothers and fathers had significantly less education than was the case for their white counterparts (father's education, t = 4.29, p = 0.00; mother's education, t = 3.19, p = 0.002). There were also differences in father's occupational level: more whites than blacks reported their fathers held white collar jobs (29.8 percent versus 7.9 percent) or were skilled laborers (22.6 percent versus 11.3 percent). By contrast, more black respondents described their fathers as unskilled laborers (23 percent) than whites (7.1 percent). Similarly, black respondents reported that their mothers held white collar positions less frequently than white respondents (17.2 percent versus 28.6 percent). On the other hand, the mothers of black respondents were much more likely to hold service or private household positions than was the case for whites (44.6 percent versus 19.7 percent).

Blacks were also more likely to have been raised in an urban environment: 85.6 percent of blacks and a mere 48.8 percent of whites reported having lived in the city during adolescence (age twelve to sixteen). Blacks more frequently reported living in the city at the time of the study as well (91 percent versus 57.7 percent). This suggests that blacks were more likely to live under 'disorganized' conditions of heterogeneity and mobility associated with urban neighborhoods. By contrast, the white respondents seemed to report more detachment from social bonds. For one thing, whites were more likely to have been moved around to different people while growing up than blacks (19.6 percent versus 8.3 percent). This suggests that familial supervision may have been undermined. Further, while both groups were about equal in the number of those reporting poor relations with their fathers (16.6 percent of whites and 14.2 percent of blacks), whites were more likely to report poor relations with their mothers than blacks (21.4 percent versus 5.4 percent). In addition, whites were slightly more likely to report that their families moved more than five times during their adolescence than blacks (33.9 percent versus 27.5 percent), which suggests familial controls may have been weakened because families were not rooted in the community. Finally, there was some evidence that white respondents may have been more detached from educational institutions while growing up than blacks: more of them described themselves as poor students (20.8 percent versus 7.8 percent).

There were some similarities by race in terms of marital status: 18.1 percent of the blacks and 21.4 percent of the whites were married at the time of the study. Educational levels were also similar: both groups had approximately eleven years of schooling. There were differences in work status: more blacks were unemployed (83.3 percent versus 73.2 percent), although the overwhelming majority of both groups did not hold jobs during the survey period. (While these figures seem high, the national population of all clients admitted to federally funded treatment programs in the survey period—1977—reports 70 percent unemployment [National Institute on Drug Abuse, 1978]). There is also evidence that the respondents' job histories were unstable, as blacks had worked on the average only 7.48 months in the two years prior to the study and whites had worked only 8.66 months.

Given their low levels of labor-force participation, it seems unlikely that many of these respondents would be able to support their deviant life-styles with monies from employment alone. Not surprisingly, then, many reported other sources of legitimate income: 36.8 percent of black users and 22.6 percent of white users supplemented their income with welfare. Some 8.7 percent of blacks and 16.1 percent of whites also received unemployment benefits, while fully 40.2 percent of blacks and 43.5 percent of whites were supported by others. Indeed, when all sources of legal income were considered—wages, welfare, unemployment benefits, pensions, support from others—81.9 percent of blacks and 79.4 percent of whites claimed at least one source of legal income.

These respondents also seem to derive much of their money from illegal income: 86.3 percent of black users and 94 percent of white users report that they have committed at least one offense on a single occasion. When the broad offense categories of prostitution, property crime, nonviolent victim crime, violent victim crime, and drug dealing are considered, the results shown in table 5.1 are obtained.

These figures indicate that a larger percentage of the white

TABLE 5.1
Illegal Activities Reported by Addicts

Type of Crime	PERCENT WHO COMMITTED CRIME AT LEAST ONCE:	
	Blacks	Whites
Prostitution	25.5%	23.2%
Property crimes	42.6%	68.3%
Drug dealing	58.8%	87.5%
Nonviolent victim crimes	29.4%	46.1%
Violent victim crimes	18.1%	22.2%

population has committed a wider range of offenses at least once. For both groups, drug dealing is the most common offense, although a substantially larger percentage of the white subsample reports this offense. This may have much to do with the concentration of white respondents in port cities such as Miami and Los Angeles, where the trade in various illegal drugs flourishes. Undoubtedly this provides them with greater access to illegal drug hierarchies than might be the case for blacks concentrated inland in a city such as Detroit.

The fact that a number of these users are involved in crime suggests involvement with deviant subcultures, and in fact 31.9 percent of blacks and 53.6 percent of whites state that their spouses or significant others have used drugs, and 40.7 percent of blacks and 50 percent of whites claim that their best friends have been users.

Data Measurement

Table 5.2 shows means, standard deviations, and brief descriptions of variables.

Dependent Variable

Some crimes committed by heroin users are not directed toward support of the habit but occur tangentially due to their constant exposure to deviant subcultures. To restrict analysis to only those crimes that allow for support of the habit, the utilitarian offense of property crime was entered as the dependent variable (ARRESTS).

TABLE 5.2
Description of Variables

Notation	Variable Name	Description	BLACKS		WHITES	
			Mean	S.D.	Mean	S.D.
X_1	RURALURB	Four-item scale measuring type of community R lived in during adolescence; high scores indicate most urban communities.	3.779	.583	3.298	.850
X_2	MOVING	Number of times R moved before age 16.	3.537	2.210	3.852	2.352
X_3	FAMORG	Dummy variable—living with *different* people coded 1; living with the *same* people coded 0.	.083	.277	.196	.398
X_4	PAASSOC	Three-point scale measuring quality of R's interaction with father; high scores indicate poor interaction.	1.490	.733	1.440	.764
X_5	MAASSOC	Three-point scale measuring quality of R's interaction with mother; high scores indicate poor interaction.	1.127	.469	1.440	.824
X_6	SCHLORG	Three-point scale measuring whether R was a poor, average, or good student in adolescence; high scores indicate good students.	2.294	.605	2.143	.736
X_7	COHABITANTS	Number of deviant behaviors committed by R's cohabitants.	.309	.864	.720	1.088
X_8	SIGOTHERUSE	Item measuring whether R's spouse or significant other uses drugs; high scores indicate drug use.	1.080	1.270	1.500	1.781

X_9	DRUGSOURCE	Three-point scale measuring source of R's preferred drug; high scores indicate most illegal source.	2.283	.555	2.307	.570
X_{10}	CONFORMITY	Scale measuring R's responsiveness to peer pressures; high scores indicate greater responsiveness.	7.054	2.872	7.449	3.201
X_{11}	PAOCCU	Census occupation categories of job held by father.	9.574	4.555	6.917	5.214
X_{12}	MAOCCU	Census occupation categories of job held by mother.	10.294	4.335	8.875	4.900
X_{13}	ACCOUNT	Scale measuring R's neutralization of drug use by blaming peers or difficult problems; high scores indicate neutralization.	2.446	.717	2.452	.724
X_{14}	JUSTICE	Item measuring neutralization through condemnation of condemners (court system); high scores indicate neutralization.	.658	.475	.719	.451
X_{15}	STUDENT	Dummy variable: yes = 1; no = 0.	.099	.299	.054	.226
X_{16}	RELIGION	Dummy variable: some religious experience = 1; no religious experience = 0.	.431	.496	.310	.464
X_{17}	ALLMONEY	Dummy variable: legitimate income = 1; no legitimate income = 0.	.819	.386	.794	.406
Y_1	ARRESTS	Number of arrests for property crimes.	1.044	2.891	1.440	2.861

Measures of variations in property crime rates have traditionally been based on self-reported rates of commission. However, many of these respondents commit crimes on a daily basis and this raises problems with the accuracy of recall if rates of commission are used. Hence, crime rates are based on self-reported arrest rates.

Independent Variables

Measuring Social Disorganization. In part, social disorganization theorists argue that community disorganization is a crucial basis for criminality, with more heterogeneous and mobile communities—that is, urban communities—being subject to more disorganization. To test community disorganization, respondents were asked what type of community they lived in during adolescence (age twelve to sixteen). Communities were then ranked from the most rural to the most urban (RURALURB). Family instability or disorganization was gauged by determining the degree to which the respondent's family was attached to or rooted in the community. Hence, respondents were asked to report the number of times their families had moved before the respondent was sixteen (MOVING).

Measuring Social Bond Theory. Attachment to family and degree of familial supervision was measured by the stability of family relationships during adolescence, so respondents were asked to report if they had always lived with the same or different people when growing up (FAMORG). FAMORG was treated as a dummy variable with family disorganization (living with different people) coded as 1 and family organization coded as 0. Attachment to the family was also measured by the quality of the relationship between respondents and their parents. Respondents were asked if they had had positive, negative, or no interaction with each parent (PAASSOC, MAASSOC). Finally, the effects of attachment to school were determined by user investment in educational attainments, so respondents were asked if they had been poor, average, or good students (SCHLORG).

Measuring Differential Association/Social Learning Theories. Differential association theorists argue that frequent contact with other deviants is crucial. To determine variations in exposure to criminals and criminal behavior patterns, respondents were asked if those who lived with them were involved in deviant behavior (for example, drug use, alcoholism, etc.). The total number of deviant behaviors committed by cohabitants was computed and used as an indicator of differential association (COHABITANTS). The effects of differential association were also based upon whether the spouse or significant other of the respondent had ever used drugs (SIGOTHERUSE); high scores indicate that the respondent had a spouse or significant other who had used heroin. Variations in exposure to deviant behavior patterns were also measured by examining the manner in which the respondent's preferred drug (usually heroin) was obtained (DRUGSOURCE). Responses indicating a reliance on legal sources or forged prescriptions for drugs were coded 1, since this suggests fewer contacts with deviant subcultures than receiving drugs as a gift from other users (coded 2) or purchasing drugs in street black markets (coded 3). Finally, to determine to what extent deviant behavior was a response to peer reinforcements, respondents were asked if they had used various drugs for peer acceptance (CONFORMITY). High scores on this variable indicate those respondents whose deviance was a response to peer reinforcements. As such, it allows for a test of social learning theory.

Measuring Social Class of Origin. A full test of social disorganization theory requires some consideration of the effects of class of origin. Class was measured by parental occupational levels (PAOCCU, MAOCCU).[1]

Measuring Neutralization Theory. Neutralization theorists argue that involvement in crime is often accompanied by explaining away the offending behavior. Crimes are explained away by suggesting that outside forces push or compel the offender to deviate. Respondents were allowed to excuse their drug use by arguing that peers or difficult problems had brought about their addiction (ACCOUNT). High scores indicate those respondents who are most inclined to neutralize.

Apart from blaming external conditions, deviants also excuse crimes by condemning those who would condemn them (for example, the court system). Hence, respondents were asked whether or not the poor had an equal chance in court, with responses suggesting an equal chance regardless of class being coded 0, and those indicating discrimination against the poor coded 1 (JUSTICE).

Measuring Commitment to Conventional Institutions. Respondent involvement in conventional institutions was measured by determining the degree of user contact with educational and religious institutions. The extent of their reliance on legal sources of income was also determined. Hence respondents were asked if they were students at the time of the survey (STUDENT). STUDENT was treated as a dummy variable with 'yes' responses coded 1 and 'no' responses coded 0. Religious involvement was gauged by asking respondents if they had had a religious experience since the age of twelve, with some religious experience coded 1 and no religious experience coded 0 (RELIGION). Since many of the respondents were unemployed, a measure including all legal sources of income was developed (ALLMONEY). Respondent access to legitimate income was computed by combining receipt of wages, welfare, unemployment benefits, pensions and/or support from others into a single measure, with receipt of legal income coded 1 and no legal income coded 0.

Results

A total of 372 respondents were interviewed and 326 interviews were sufficiently complete to be included in the regression analysis. There were no significant differences between those with complete and incomplete interviews in terms of race, age, and gender.

To determine if there were problems with multi-collinearity, a correlation matrix was generated for all of the independent variables (see table 5.3). As none of the correlations exceeded 0.50, multi-collinearity is not expected to affect the analysis.

The results from regression of ARRESTS for property crimes on the independent variables appear in table 5.4, and the unique contribution of each theoretical category of predictors is presented in table 5.5.

Blacks

Separate regressions were run for blacks and whites and in the equation for blacks, some 18.6 percent of the variance ($r^2 = .18576$) was explained. When the unique contribution of each theoretical subset is examined, it is clear that only social disorganization/social bond theory predictors account for a significant amount of the

TABLE 5.3
Correlation Matrix for Independent Variables
(Blacks above Diagonal, Whites below Diagonal)

	X_1	X_2	X_3	X_4	X_5	X_6	X_7	X_8	X_9	X_{10}	X_{11}	X_{12}	X_{13}	X_{14}	X_{15}	X_{16}	X_{17}
X_1	1.00	.06	.08	-.12	.10	-.07	-.10	.02	-.07	-.04	.02	-.07	-.06	.01	.03	-.09	.01
X_2	-.08	1.00	.12	-.15	-.01	-.07	.01	.03	-.08	.04	.14	.08	.01	.10	.14	.20	.15
X_3	.04	.39	1.00	-.03	-.04	-.05	-.08	.09	.04	.05	-.01	.07	.03	.09	-.10	-.06	.04
X_4	.04	.09	.10	1.00	.16	.01	-.01	-.04	.15	.05	.36	.19	.06	-.06	-.01	-.16	-.14
X_5	-.14	.16	.05	.09	1.00	.08	.02	-.07	-.25	.03	.04	.07	-.07	.06	-.01	-.04	.07
X_6	.01	-.02	.09	-.16	-.01	1.00	-.05	.06	.08	-.05	-.13	-.01	-.02	-.12	-.05	.02	.13
X_7	.00	.01	.01	.00	-.06	.04	1.00	.25	-.01	.07	.03	-.12	-.04	.07	-.07	-.01	.09
X_8	-.07	-.01	-.05	-.27	-.03	-.02	.35	1.00	.03	.02	-.11	-.04	-.02	-.05	.04	.06	.02
X_9	.05	-.08	-.05	.06	-.06	.03	-.04	.00	1.00	-.01	.19	-.01	.10	-.07	-.16	.04	.01
X_{10}	.11	-.16	.03	-.06	-.17	-.02	-.03	-.09	.04	1.00	.01	-.13	.00	-.13	-.04	.01	-.19
X_{11}	-.01	.11	.13	.26	.21	.01	.10	-.01	-.10	-.10	1.00	.33	.09	.06	-.02	-.09	-.04
X_{12}	.05	-.07	.10	.03	.10	.13	-.12	-.10	-.08	-.05	-.01	1.00	.03	.01	.04	.04	-.01
X_{13}	.06	.18	.14	.12	.07	.13	-.02	-.09	-.03	.00	.00	.12	1.00	.08	.01	-.14	.03
X_{14}	-.13	.08	.00	-.08	.04	-.03	.11	-.02	.02	.00	.06	.02	.02	1.00	.01	-.11	.11
X_{15}	.10	-.01	-.04	-.14	.02	.19	.02	-.02	-.04	-.02	-.01	-.04	-.07	-.06	1.00	.19	.18
X_{16}	-.05	-.02	.07	.01	-.07	.17	.14	.10	.01	-.07	.01	-.14	.01	.17	-.03	1.00	.04
X_{17}	-.02	-.28	-.10	.03	-.10	.06	.02	.03	-.11	.01	-.02	-.10	-.07	.17	.12	.04	1.00

Key to Variable Notations

X_1 = RURALURB X_6 = SCHLORG X_{10} = CONFORMITY X_{14} = JUSTICE
X_2 = MOVING X_7 = COHABITANTS X_{11} = PAOCCU X_{15} = STUDENT
X_3 = FAMORG X_8 = SIGOTHERUSE X_{12} = MAOCCU X_{16} = RELIGION
X_4 = PAASSOC X_9 = DRUGSOURCE X_{13} = ACCOUNT X_{17} = ALLMONEY
X_5 = MAASSOC

TABLE 5.4
Regression of Arrests on Independent Variables

Variable	BLACKS		WHITES	
	Beta	F/(Sig. F)	Beta	F/(Sig. F)
Social disorganization/social bond				
RURALURB	.030	.166 (n.s.)	.083	.966 (n.s.)
MOVING	.190*	6.232 (.014)	−.174	3.199 (n.s.)
FAMORG	.193**	6.933 (.009)	.016	.029 (n.s.)
PAASSOC	.058	.522 (n.s.)	−.055	.342 (n.s.)
MAASSOC	.103	1.851 (n.s.)	.053	.377 (n.s.)
SCHLORG	−.199**	7.394 (.007)	−.137	2.376 (n.s.)
Differential association/social learning				
COHABITANTS	.032	.175 (n.s.)	.229*	6.559 (.012)
SIGOTHERUSE	−.105	2.009 (n.s.)	.107	1.333 (n.s.)
DRUGSOURCE	−.046	.350 (n.s.)	−.045	.288 (n.s.)
CONFORMITY	.112	2.326 (n.s.)	.179*	4.402 (.038)
Social class background				
PAOCCU	−.087	1.095 (n.s.)	−.056	.404 (n.s.)
MAOCCU	−.008	.010 (n.s.)	.109	1.558 (n.s.)
Neutralization				
ACCOUNT	.026	.134 (n.s.)	.077	.803 (n.s.)
JUSTICE	−.104	2.017 (n.s.)	.068	.611 (n.s.)
Commitment to conventional institutions				
STUDENT	−.092	1.538 (n.s.)	−.053	.382 (n.s.)
RELIGION	.046	.358 (n.s.)	−.085	.951 (n.s.)
ALLMONEY	−.078	1.059 (n.s.)	−.002	.001 (n.s.)
(CONSTANT)	1.641	(n.s.)	2.379	(n.s.)
N	185	141		
R2	.18576	.18693		

*   significant at the 0.05 level
**   significant at the 0.01 level

explained variance ($r^2 = .1259$). This is due largely to three predictors, MOVING, SCHLORG, and FAMORG. Consistent with these theories, the significant betas for FAMORG and MOVING indicate that those respondents who were subjected to less supervision are more likely to be involved in crime to support their habits. That is, those users who were moved around to different relatives and those whose families moved a lot report higher arrest rates. Similarly, those respondents who describe themselves as poor students (SCHLORG) are more likely to be involved in crime.

TABLE 5.5
Unique Contribution of Each Category of Predictors for Arrests

Category	Number of Measures in the Set	Unique Contribution Blacks	Whites
Social disorg./soc. bond	6	.1259	.0540
Diff. assoc./soc. learning	4	.0237	.1138
Social class	2	.0062	.0136
Neutralization	2	.0102	.0095
Commitment to conventional institutions	3	.0144	.0085
All predictors		.18576	.18693

Note: The unique contribution of a set of predictors is the gain in R2 achieved when that set is added to the regression equation after all other predictors have already been entered in the equation.

The remaining theoretical subsets—differential association/social learning, neutralization, social class, and commitment—accounted for little of the explained variance and the separate predictors within these categories were not significant.

Whites

All of the predictors account for about one-fifth of the variance (r^2 = .18693) for white respondents, which is comparable to the amount explained in the equation for blacks. The predictors that test differential association/social learning theories make the single largest contribution to variance explained (r^2 = .1138) due to the strength of two variables, COHABITANTS and CONFORMITY. The relationship between COHABITANTS and property crimes suggests that users who report having more deviant cohabitants are themselves more likely to be involved in criminal acts. Similarly, those users who report a greater willingness to deviate in the face of peer pressures (CONFORMITY) are significantly more likely to commit property crimes. The other categories—social disorganization/social bond, neutralization, social class, and commitment—explain only a small percentage of the variance, and none of the separate predictors within these categories is significant.

Summary and Discussion

Regression analysis indicates that social disorganization or social bond predictors have a notable impact upon offense levels among blacks, while they have no impact on criminality among whites. At first glance, this might suggest that black overrepresentation in 'disorganized' urban areas is having an effect. However, the type of community in which these users resided (urban versus suburban) had no impact on criminality. At best, then, community conditions may operate through other institutions. With blacks, it was argued that a history of crime containment, poor relationships between the community and police, and the juxtaposition of stable families with populations of unattached males may mean that a large number of black youth have ready access to well-developed drug and criminal street subcultures. Hence, breakdowns in familial or school supervision were expected to have more impact upon crime among blacks than whites. This is borne out, since blacks who experienced reduced familial and school supervision as juveniles report significantly higher crime rates than those who did not. By contrast, measures of weakened supervision and detachment from family and school had no impact on whites, despite the fact that whites showed higher levels of detachment on certain of these measures. An alternative explanation suggests itself, in that blacks may have been more likely to have been arrested in their juvenile years when they reported poor family supervision or detachment from the school than whites (Werthman and Piliavin, 1967; Cicourel, 1968); hence, an artificial correlation between crime and disorganization would have been created.

Community conditions may also affect levels of criminality among whites indirectly by operating through other microlevel conditions. White users—particularly those in suburban areas— may have lacked widespread access to the street drug and criminal subcultures available to blacks, so mere reductions in familial and school supervision would not have been sufficient to expose them to deviant opportunities. Indeed, white users, on average, reported earlier experimentation with illegal drugs including heroin than blacks, and yet, despite this evidence of early detachment from family and school surveillance, these measures of weakened bonds had no effect. In the absence of well-developed street cultures, many of these mid-1970s users may have had to seek out others involved in drugs and deviance. Under these conditions, then, differential association with other drug-using and criminal populations may have been crucial in their initiation and maintenance of drug and criminal careers. This receives some support, as differential association and social learning predictors have significant effect on their levels of criminality, while these predictors have no influence on blacks.

Interestingly, social class of origin had no effect on levels of criminality for either group. Perhaps measures of class based on mother's and father's occupational levels might have been expected to have more of an effect in a sample of juveniles than in this young-adult population. There was also no evidence of racial differences in neutralizations, as these accounts had no significant impact on crime levels for either blacks or whites. This may suggest that these accounts are only important in the early stages of the career when the initial break with conventional society occurs. As the career progresses and crime becomes routine, excusing and justifying these acts may no longer be required. Since the users in this sample are young adults in the midst of their careers, deviant acts may indeed have been routinized and the need for neutralization eliminated.

Finally, evidence of commitment to conventional institutions was expected to have some influence on offense levels. Indeed, the effect was presumed to be great in this young-adult criminal sample, as commitment to these institutions has implications for maintenance of criminal careers. In particular, evidence of employment was supposed to have some effect, as it is presumed to draw criminals away from crime. Employment and access to legal sources of income were expected to have this effect because they provide a stake in conformity so that offenders are less willing to risk arrest. However, access to legal sources of income were not shown to have any effect on crime for either blacks or whites. The fact that the overwhelming majority of both black and white users were unemployed at the time of the survey and reported unstable work histories might account for this finding. Clearly, the capacity of employment to provide a stake in conformity through occupational socialization, self-esteem, and limiting time available for illegal pursuits is undermined when the potential offenders are rarely employed or employed in menial positions. The tenuousness of the ties that these respondents have to the labor force, then, undoubtedly limits the importance of employment or legal sources of income.

Note

1. Respondents were asked the following questions about their parents' occupations:

   • What kind of job did your father (or the man who raised you) usually have, if any? If he had more than one job, just tell me his main job. (See categories below.)
   • What kind of job did your mother (or the woman who raised you) usually have, if any? If she had more than one job, just tell me her main job. (See categories below.)

   Their options were the categories from the "Occupational Classifical System" on pages *x–xiv* of the *Classified Index of Industries and Occupations* (1970 Census of Population, U.S. Department of Commerce), which were recoded in the following manner:

> 1 Professional, technical, and kindred
> 2 Managers
> 3 Clerical
> 4 Skilled labor
> 5 Military
> 6 Operatives
> 7 Transport operatives
> 8 Unskilled labor
> 9 Farm managers

References

Akers, R. 1977. *Deviant Behavior: A Social Learning Approach.* 2nd ed. Belmont, Mass.: Wadsworth.

Akers, R., M. D. Krohn, L. Lanze-Kaduce, and M. Radosevich. 1979. "Social Learning and Deviant Behavior: A Specific Test of a General Theory." *American Sociological Review* 44:635–55.

Ball, J. 1970. "Two Patterns of Opiate Addiction." In *The Epidemiology of Opiate Addiction in the United States,* edited by J. Ball and C. Chambers. Springfield, Ill.: Charles Thomas.

Berk, R. A., K. J. Lenihan, and P. Rossi. 1980. "Crime and Poverty: Some Experimental Evidence from Ex-Offenders." *American Sociological Review* 45:766–86.

Best, J., and D. Luckenbill. 1982. *Organizing Deviance.* Englewood Cliffs: Prentice-Hall.

Bursik, R. J., and J. Webb. 1982. "Community Change and Patterns of Delinquency." *American Journal of Sociology* 88:24–43.

Calvin, A. D. 1981. "Unemployment among Black Youths, Demographics and Crime." *Crime and Delinquency* 27:234–44.

Chein, I. D. Gerard, R. Lee, and E. Rosenfeld. 1964. *The Road to H.* New York: Basic Books.

Clinard, M. 1968. *Sociology of Deviant Behavior.* New York: Holt, Rinehart, and Winston.

Cicourel, A. 1968. *The Social Organization of Juvenile Justice.* New York: Wiley.

Covington, J. 1979. "The Creation of Deviant Self." Unpublished dissertation, University of Chicago.

———. 1986. "Self-Esteem and Deviance: The Effects of Race and Gender." *Criminology* 24:105–38.

———. 1987. "Addict Attitudes toward Legalization of Heroin." *Contemporary Drug Problems* 14:315–53.

Diprete, T. A. 1981. "Unemployment over the Life Cycle: Racial Differences and the Effects of Changing Economic Conditions." *American Journal of Sociology* 87:286–307.

Elliott, D. S., D. Huizinga, and S. Ageton. 1985. *Explaining Delinquency and Drug Use.* Beverly Hills: Sage.

Faris, R. 1948. *Social Disorganization.* New York: The Ronald Press.

Ginsberg, I., and J. R. Greeley. 1978. "Competing Theories of Marihuana Use: A Longitudinal Study." *Journal of Health and Social Behavior* 19:22–34.

Hagan, J., and C. Albonetti. 1982. "Race, Class, and the Perception of Criminal Injustice in America." *American Journal of Sociology* 88:329–55.

Hahn, H. 1971. "Ghetto Assessments of Police Protection and Authority." *Law and Society Review* 6:183–94.

Hannerz, U. 1969. *Soulside: Inquiries into Ghetto Culture and Community.* New York: Columbia University Press.

Hirschi, T. 1969. *Causes of Delinquency.* Berkeley: University of California Press.

Holzman, H. 1982. "The Rationalistic Opportunity Perspective on Criminal Behavior: Toward a Reformulation of the Theoretical Basis for the Notion of Property Crime as Work." *Crime and Delinquency* 28:233–46.

Homans, G. 1950. *The Human Group.* New York: Harcourt, Brace, and Jovanovich.

Hughes, P., and G. Crawford. 1974. "Epidemiology of Heroin Addiction in the 1970s: New Opportunities and Responsibilities." In *Drug Use:*

Epidemiological and Sociological Approaches, edited by E. Josephson and E. Carroll. Washington, D.C.: Hemisphere Publishing.

Jacob, H. 1971. "Black and White Perceptions of Justice in the City." *Law and Society Review* 6:69–89.

Johnston, L., P. O'Malley, and J. Bachman. 1986. *Drug Use among American High School Students, College Students, and Other Young Adults.* Rockville, Md.: National Institute on Drug Abuse.

Knox, G. 1981. "Differential Integration and Job Retention among Ex-Offenders." *Criminology* 18:481–99.

Kornhauser, R. R. 1978. *Social Sources of Delinquency.* Chicago: University of Chicago Press.

Liebow, E. 1967. *Tally's Corner.* Boston: Little, Brown, and Company.

Liker, J. K. 1982. "Wage and Status Effects of Employment on Affective Well-Being Among Ex-Felons." *American Sociological Review* 47:264–83.

Luckenbill, D., and J. Best. 1981. "Careers in Deviance and Respectability: The Analogy's Limitations." *Social Problems* 29:197–206.

Minor, W. W. 1981. "Techniques of Neutralization: A Reconceptualization and Empirical Examination." *Journal of Research in Crime and Delinquency* 18:295–318.

National Institute on Drug Abuse. 1978. Division of Scientific and Program Information. *SMSA Statistics: Data from the Client Oriented Data Acquisition Process.* Rockville, Md.: National Institute on Drug Abuse.

Shaw, C., and H. McKay. 1972. *Juvenile Delinquency and Urban Areas.* Chicago: University of Chicago Press.

Spear, A. 1968. *Black Chicago: The Making of a Negro Ghetto.* Chicago: University of Chicago Press.

Spergel, I. 1984. "Violent Gangs in Chicago: In Search of Social Policy." *Social Service Review* 58:199–226.

Staff of *Newsday.* 1974. *The Heroin Trail.* New York: Signet.

Sutherland, E., and D. Cressey. 1955. *Principles of Criminology.* Philadelphia: J. B. Lippincott.

Sviridoff, M., and J. Thompson. 1983. "Links between Employment and Crime: A Qualitative Study of Rikers Island Releasees." *Crime and Delinquency* 29:195–212.

Sykes, G., and D. Matza. 1957. "Techniques of Neutralization: A Theory of Delinquency." *American Sociological Review* 22:664–70.

Thornberry, T., and M. Farnsworth. 1982. "Social Correlates of Criminal Involvement: Further Evidence on the Relationship between Social Status and Criminal Behavior." *American Sociological Review* 46:525–41.

Werthman, C., and I. Piliavin. 1967. "Gang Members and Ecological Conflict." In *The Police,* edited by D. J. Bordua. New York: Wiley.

Wilson, W. 1978. *The Declining Significance of Race.* Chicago: University of Chicago Press.

Yablonsky, L. 1970. *The Violent Gang.* Baltimore: Penguin.

6

The Media World of Crime: A Study of Social Learning Theory and Symbolic Interaction

Hans Joachim Schneider

The Significance of the Topic

During the last decade, the mass media have grown larger, more influential, and more powerful worldwide. In the Federal Republic of Germany, during the 1950s, viewers could receive but one TV channel; in the 1960s and 1970s they were able to receive three, and the number of available TV channels has risen to eleven or even more in the last few years, especially through cable TV. And even more TV channels are to come. Cable News Network and similar ventures have made instant, worldwide television exposure a reality. Additionally, there are huge numbers of videos, and the distribution of video recorders in the population is increasing rapidly. Worldwide, we are on the way to a communication-conditioned mass-media society in which fiction, fantasy, and the definition of reality assume a greater role than reality itself, where people want to be permanently entertained, and where the portrayal of the contents gains more emphasis than the contents themselves.

For centuries news on crime has fascinated people. In the Middle Ages ballad singers moved deftly from town to town in order to spread their ballads, which, to a great extent, were stories of murder and illicit love. Crime stories are not a novelty, because they do not report anything really new. They are regularly told according to the pattern of the "familiar sensation," because they have a function of relief for the society, because through them, the "law-abiding citizen" can set himself apart from the criminal, because they prove to him that his identity is "normal," and because he can be content to feel that he is better than the criminals, and that he successfully managed to escape the criminal act (Reiwald, 1948; Ostermeyer, 1975). People hunger for news about crime, because it is entertaining and banishes the boredom of everyday life. The mass media willingly fulfill this demand, because news about crime is cheap, it is easy to get hold of, and it helps sell almost any product. Therefore, there is a symbiosis, an unholy alliance, between the mass media and society, against which the discerning criminologist advances his objections virtually in vain.

The Example of an Empirical Case Study

In 1922, M. K. Wisehart was the first to discover that the mass media (through "publicized opinion") influenced public perception of crime and criminal justice, although neither mass media portrayals ("public opinion") were in accordance with the reality of crime as expressed in crime statistics and criminological research. The reality of crime and criminal justice in criminological research is a construct as well. It raises the epistemological question whether we really perceive the things we mean to perceive. It is, moreover, based on the concept of social perception, which assumes that everything we perceive is strongly influenced by the society in which we live. Apart from these theoretical and methodological problems, which have to be faced by every kind of research, the criminological construct of the reality of crime and criminal justice is, as a rule, incomparably more reliable and valid than the media's portrayal of crime and criminal justice. Since Wisehart's time, the social-psychological mechanism he discovered has been confirmed in numerous empirical research studies (Davis, 1952; Jones, 1976; Humphries, 1981). One of the most recent studies was published in New Zealand (Kelsey and Young, 1982).

The thesis that the portrayals of crime and criminal justice in the media and public opinion are constantly influencing each other, and that criminological research on the reality of crime has almost no impact on either publicized opinion or public opinion was demonstrated by Mark Fishman (1978): the mass media produce "crime waves," subjective impressions of periodic outbreaks of epidemics of criminal offenses. In late 1976, New York City experienced such a media crime wave. Three newspapers, the *New York Times,* the *New York Daily News,* and the *New York Post,* as well as the five local television networks, reported case after case of violent crimes against elderly people. The audience received the impression that crimes against elderly people were increasing. This media crime wave lasted for about seven weeks. Newspapers and television networks all over the United States took notice of it. "Crimes against the elderly" were typical crimes with typical victims, typical offenders, and typical circumstances. The perpetrators of robbery, murder, and rape against elderly people were in most cases young minority-group people with long juvenile records. They came from ghetto neighborhoods, near residential areas for elderly white people, the typical victims, who for various reasons, mostly poverty, had not fled the inner city of New York City for the suburbs. The journalists used the concept of "crime against the elderly" like a film script, and during November and December, 1976, they reported one brutal incident after another.

The media crime wave had no factual basis whatsover. The crime statistics of the New York City Police Department did not show any increase in crimes against elderly people for November/December of 1976. As a matter of fact, for murder of elderly people, the crime statistics even showed a decline of 19 percent compared to the previous year. Even though in the New York City police statistics, murder of elderly people accounted for a rate of less than 1 percent, 28 percent of the crime news referred to murder of elderly people. The crimes against elderly people in 1976 differed in no way from the crime trends of the general population (Fishman, 1978). Although the media crime wave had no basis in reality, it nevertheless caused an interaction between publicized opinion and public opinion. Opinion polls in the United States in May 1977 showed that 60 percent of the respondents stated their opinion that crimes against the elderly had risen in number. Half of the respondents over fifty years of age feared that they might not be as safe in the streets as one year ago (Fishman, 1978). As soon as the mass media had "invented" a crime theme for their reporting, they also reported the reactions, which they themselves had caused. In this sense, mass media "create" their own crime news. Publicized opinion and public opinion have a mutual influence on each other; they interact constantly. The mass media do not merely reflect the social process they inform about. Rather, they interfere with the social process by creating reactions to their news and reporting about those reactions. Reform proposals for the criminal justice system are made. Questions and debates are on the parliamentary agenda. New police programs are instituted, and citizens' meetings are held. The official reactions make the "crime wave" seem even more believable than it was on the basis of media reports. By means of selective reporting, the mass media direct social awareness and shape social visibility of crime according to their own needs, not according to criminological research or the needs of social control.

The media crime waves may be only imaginary, the result of interaction between publicized opinion and public opinion, but they have consequences in social reality, in the administration of justice, and even in penal legislation. This became visible during the media crime wave at the end of 1976 in New York City. The juvenile court system was criticized. Juvenile courts and training schools were considered too lenient and too indulgent. Under the impact of public opinion, juvenile courts and training schools altered their practices: they inflicted more severe sentences, and they executed them more relentlessly. Bills aiming at increasing penalties for juvenile offenders with long juvenile records who had committed a crime against an elderly person were submitted to the New York State legislature (Fishman, 1978).

The reason that media crime waves are created is quite simple: journalists approach the abundance of crime news with thematic propositions. The news theme becomes, for some time, the selective criterion and unifying concept around which news items are grouped; news items are generally reported only if they correspond to a trend in crime and social control—real or alleged, past or only just beginning. "Media crime waves" result from the interaction between news organizations. In search of "the crime news of the day," all competitors do the same thing: they read, listen to, and view each other, and they use the same sources of news: news agency reports, press releases, and police news dispatches. Police press offices cooperate with the mass media in the creation of media crime waves insofar as they supply the mass media with crime news that they assume to be of interest to the public and therefore suitable for mass media presentation.

The Theoretical Bases: Social Learning Theory and Symbolic Interaction

The thesis that the portrayal of criminality and criminal justice results in consequences in personal as well as in social reality rests, first of all, on social learning theory (Bandura, 1977). According to this theory, behavior is learned not only according to its success, but also through observation of models, that is, through "substitutory" experience. People "create," through their behavior, social conditions that, in turn, affect their behavior. People learn not only behavioral modes, but also attitudes and justifications for their behavior from social stereotypes and prejudices. Most of all, they learn through processes of self-encouragement in which the measure of self-reward and self-punishment may again result from social prejudices. They follow value notions and behavioral styles, because they assume that the majority of the population considers them to be correct. The mass media adjust themselves to such value notions of public opinion, but they shape them as well; they both form and deform social behavior.

The thesis that the portrayal of criminality and criminal justice results in consequences in personal as well as in social reality can, on the other hand, be traced back to the theory of symbolic interaction (Mead, 1976; Blumer, 1972). In the interaction between mass media and public opinion, what kind of *meaning* the mass media attribute to socially deviant and criminal behavior, that is, how they interpret them, is important. The media do, after all, influence the societal stereotypes, which, in turn, enter human interaction as interpretation. The mass media alienate the phenomenon of criminality from society. People nurse pictures of criminality and criminals that do not correspond to the reality of crime. Such pictures result from prejudices and conceptual clichés that the mass media produce and that people believe in because they do not have any experience with the violent crimes that are depicted. The distance reaction of the mass media, their "projecting into remote distance," and their concept of the criminal as the "bad guy" contribute to a change in the definition and the self-definition of the law violator, and both reinforce and accelerate the process of alienation from society. The law violator adopts the picture that he thinks society holds of him. The constructed image of criminality and criminal justice becomes the measure that defines everyday criminal situations in society, and that develops attitudes toward criminals, criminal justice, and the effectiveness of social control. Constructed reality becomes reality, because we believe in it and adjust our behavior accordingly.

Media Portrayal of Crime and Criminal Justice

Numerous content analysts have conducted analytic research on the form and content of crime portrayal in TV news programs (Roshier, 1973; Chibnall, 1977; Dominick, 1973, 1978; Humphries, 1981; Sherizen, 1978), reports, documentaries, "search and seizure" programs, entertainment programs (Schneider, 1977, 1979a, 1979b, 1980, 1981, 1982, 1987; Stein-Hilbers, 1976; Jubelius, 1981; Pandiani, 1978), and in serious newspapers, yellow-press publications, and, especially, in caricatures, comics, and court reports in newspapers. Of utmost importance are the TV entertainment programs about crime (detective stories, Westerns), since these are broadcast in prime time and enjoy high audience ratings, and since they far outnumber any informational TV programs on criminality. Moreover, they appeal intensively to both hearing and seeing. Their contents are completely detached from the reality of crime.

Crime news and documentaries are incapable of correcting the portrayal of crime in entertainment programs in terms of a stronger reality orientation. Documentaries are presented predominantly as peripheral programming: they are broadcast at less favorable times (late night) or on local networks and are directed mainly at an educated audience in their presentation (language, high degree of abstraction). In addition to this, they rarely try to make crime understandable as a normal, everyday phenomenon (proximity perspective). Documentaries, on the contrary, often employ the principle of entertainment in trying to make crime look interesting as something extraordinary, thus frequently supplementing, supporting, and enlarging the entertaining crime portrayal (remote perspective). The same is true for TV news and for crime reporting in serious newspapers. These differ from TV entertainment and the yellow press only in terms of the form, not the contents of their crime reporting.

As crime reports and crime entertainment programs appear on the TV screen in the form of a variety program, and as crime entertainment programs frequently try to create the impression of reality, the recipient with an average education is almost incapable of distinguishing between facts and fiction, even more so as the contents of crime report and crime entertainment are practically identical.

Content analyses render conclusively a fairly uniform picture of crime, which the mass media distribute with remarkable continuity, and which they correct only insufficiently.

- Media criminality is almost exclusively violent crime between strangers. There is no portrayal of violence in the family, or among relatives, friends, neighbors, and acquaintances. Neither is it demonstrated that violent crimes, for example criminal homicide, develop in interaction processes between perpetrators and victims, who often know each other and in many cases share a more or less intense emotional relationship. Violence is presented in an embellished, aesthetically appealing fashion. The negative consequences of violence are ignored. The very frequent traffic violations, property crimes, and economic crimes are but minor subjects in the mass media.
- The crime portrayal in the mass media concentrates on the perpetration and the detection of the offense. It is directed at events that refer, for example, to the exterior form of the offense, the prosecution, and the conviction. The development of crime prior to the perpetration itself, and the developments of the offender and the victim after the conviction of the offender, are presented but rarely. The criminal offenses are viewed through the eyes of the investigators, that is, in most cases, the police. The investigators' personal and social backgrounds, however, are hardly exposed. Likewise, events in criminal procedure or corrections are no subjects for criminality entertainment, and they are seldom taken up by crime reporting.
- In the "media world of crime," the offender is an unfair, disagreeable, reckless, and egotistical character. In most cases, he has a criminal record and plans his crimes carefully. His motives either remain obscure or are superficial greed or revenge. Under-

lying causes of law violations are not depicted. The description of the offender's personality development and his criminal career is but insufficiently differentiated. There is no information about his family background, the social position of his parents, the living conditions in his parental home, or his school performance.

- In the "media world of crime," the victim is guileless and completely surprised by the crime. The offense—generally a serious violent crime—does not develop in an interactional process between offender and victim; they neither know nor have a relationship with each other. Victims never endanger themselves; they never put themselves into victimogenous situations, where they may easily become victims of crime. The victim is passive and never provokes the offender. He is completely guiltless, not involved in the crime, helpless and wholly at the mercy of the criminal. Contrary to the offender, he is likeable and socially useful so that the viewer or reader can easily identify with the victim. Still, his personality is depicted as shapeless and colorless, and his social background is disregarded. If he suffers damage from the offense, it is practically always death. Social and psychological damages to the victim are not made visible in the mass media, and are not presented as a serious problem; thus, they are virtually unknown to the population.

- In the "media world of crime," crime control is performed almost exclusively by the formal social control organs: police, courts, and corrections. Compared to the portrayal of investigators, private detectives, and police lieutenants, the portrayal of judges, prosecutors, and correctional officials is rare. In any case, informal social control through family, school, professional, and recreational peer group, has no function. The social responsibility for crime prevention is disregarded, as are the social causes in the development of crime. Crime control is always a repressive specialists' occupation, which is depicted as highly successful. Practically all the crimes presented are detected. As the media audience is left uninformed on the enormous dark figure of hidden, unreported crime and on the low detection rate of identified offenders of property crime, he or she can indulge in a deceptive fictitious feeling of safety. The media fail to explain to their audiences that the formal social control, for example the police, can work effectively only if the informal social control, for example the family, is fundamentally intact and undisturbed.

- Neither in the personal nor in the social context do the mass media devote sufficient treatment to the causes of crime. They analyze neither the individual crime nor criminality as a mass phenomenon. In the media portrayal, the individual act of crime is set apart from its social and personal circumstances and put into conceptual processes that are artificial and alienated from reality. This "projecting into remote distance" renders criminality both dramatic, thrilling, and sensational, as well as unrealistic and incomprehensible (Hoefnagels, 1973, pp. 16–42).

Five Examples of Particular Forms of Media Crime Portrayal

The portrayal of crime in the TV news, in the TV "search and seizure" programs, and in serious newspapers, especially in caricatures and comics and in reports about court proceedings, does not—with regard to the contents—differ much from the general image of criminality outlined in the mass media, an image predominantly coined by the TV entertainment programs dealing with crimes.

News Programs

TV news programs have a high audience rating and a high authenticity. Through the selection and placement of the news they contribute to the formation of public opinion. The TV news *"Tagesschau"* (TV channel 1 in the Federal Republic of Germany) and *"Heute"* (TV channel 2) concentrate in their crime reports on the outer form of the course of events in spectacular violent crimes, both domestic and foreign, which often bear a political reference (for example, terrorism), and on their immediate results: investigation, search, detection, arrest, detention, conviction, extradition, deportation, expulsion. Although there are special TV programs, *"Tagesthemen"* (channel 1) and *"Heute Journal"* (channel 2), for the purpose of news background information, crime news reporting "for orientation" is mostly highlights that do not illuminate the background information and do not reveal the context for a better understanding (Höing, 1983; cf. also Graber, 1980).

"Investigative" TV

On the Second German TV Channel, a television series that is very popular with the TV audience and the criminal police has been running for more than twenty years. It turns the search for offenders into a kind of entertainment. The public is asked to participate in the search. This series is also broadcast in Switzerland and Austria. The series not only searches for unidentified offenders but also offers help for the clearing of crimes. In this context it publishes pictures and names of persons who have a connection with a crime—mostly violent crimes—but who have not been sentenced in a criminal procedure.

Despite its high popularity, this TV series is problematic. Television is *not* an investigative authority. Because of its collaboration with the police, this TV series is considered to be a "mouthpiece" for the police. Its ostensibly official character enhances the audience's impression that violent crimes are widespread and that the investigations of the police constitute the main element in the repression of crime. The TV series can interfere with the course of future legal proceedings because judges, especially lay judges, are negatively influenced in their attitude toward the accused by the TV portrayal (Gerald, 1983). It can complicate the rehabilitation of criminal offenders who have been identified and apprehended through this popular TV program and who, therefore, have been stigmatized before a large part of the TV audience. The TV series, which is presented by a free-lance collaborator of the Second German TV Channel but which is made with the collaboration of the police, does not offer any criminological analyses in individual cases or with regard to the development of criminality in society in general (Geerds, 1979; Schima, n.d.; Killias, 1982, p. 24).

Newspapers

A comparison of the portrayal of crime in the *Bild-Zeitung,* the largest yellow-press publication of the Federal Republic of Germany, and in the *Frankfurter Allgemeine Zeitung,* the most respected serious newspaper of Germany, showed that the portrayal of crime differed from one newspaper to the other only in terms of form, not of content. The reporting focuses on the perpetration, the detection, and the punishment of the offense. The image of criminality in both newspapers is dominated by a description of the offense that attaches too much importance to outer appearances. Unanimously, the problem of crime is presented in an abridged form. Neither newspaper devotes much attention to the criminological and criminal justice problems of the offender, the victim, and the formal social control (the police, courts, and correctional institutions). No analysis of the causation of the crime, of the perpetrator's and the victim's personalities, or of the criminal justice reaction of the courts and the correctional institutions is provided.

This result comes as a surprise, since it had generally been assumed that serious newspapers offered analyses of criminality to their readers. The portrayal of criminality in both newspapers differed only insofar as the *Bild-Zeitung* presented its crime reports in a sensational and dramatizing fashion appealing to its readers' emotions, while the *Frankfurter Allgemeine Zeitung* reported in a sober, reserved, and composed style about crime, to which it generally does not seem to attribute as much importance as does the *Bild-Zeitung* (Schwacke, 1983).

Cartoons and Comics

Criminality plays an important role in cartoons and comics, which immunize children and adolescents against feelings of sympathy and make them numb and insensitive to the sufferings of others. In cartoons and comics, criminals and noncriminals are easily recognizable by their "tabs of identity": the detectives are blonde, blue-eyed elite men; they fight inferior law violators who have evil-mindedness, envy, and jealousy written all over their faces. Law violators have bird-like, sly faces, gappy teeth with saliva dripping from them, and claw-like, gouty hands. They are characterized as inferior and repulsive by their peaked caps, their protruding cheekbones, their cauliflower ears, their unshaven faces, and their receding foreheads. In cartoons and comics, there still lives the spirit of Cesare Lombroso's criminologically refuted theory, according to which offenders may be identified by physical characteristics, criminality is hereditary, and criminality represents a retrogression into primitive epochs of the history of man (Hess and Mariner, 1975).

Courtroom Reports

An analysis of the courtroom reports of a Westphalian provincial newspaper showed that the choice of vocabulary similarly tends to stigmatize the offender. The defendant is a fiend, a "firebug," a crook, a light-finger, a have-not craving for recognition, a scoundrel, an evil cruel father, a dodger, a boozing mate. He is bad, dangerous, and dissolute. This choice of vocabulary is subjective and degrading. The reports are enriched with invectives, curses, and florid phrases. In order to create a round story, facts are omitted or invented. Anything the defendant does is wrong, ridiculous, mean, stupid, malicious, irresponsible—typically criminal. The courtroom reports of this German provincial newspaper are merely light, entertaining short stories, which paint reality in black-and-white, nothing but variations of anecdotes. They do not fulfill their tasks in terms of control of jurisdiction and analysis of crime (Ostermeyer, 1971).

Interpretation of Reality

The communicators of the mass media try to achieve suspense and entertainment by portraying criminality as something outrageous, obscure, weird, extraordinary, and miraculous. Criminality is presented as appealing and beautified. The criminal event is farcical; it stimulates a pleasant creepy feeling; it makes the moral self-satisfaction and self-conceit of the noncriminal possible; the noncriminal can thus set himself apart from the criminal. In their crime portrayal, the media still follow an outdated theory of criminality that regards the offender as a psychopath, a mentally abnormal person. In the media the offender is a monster who deserves hate and contempt. The victim of crime belongs to the untouchables, the taboo persons, whose true fate one should not be concerned with, who was victimized vicariously for all other people, who lives on the dark side of life, who might have even subconsciously wanted to be a victim of crime.

The false crime picture that the audience possesses on the basis of media crime portrayal cannot easily be corrected by the daily experience that people have with crime. Admittedly, many people become victims of crime once or even several times in their lives. There is, however, a considerable difference between the personally experienced law violation and the kind that one reads, hears about, or watches in the mass media. While immediately experienced crime consists most often of petty offenses, shoplifting and employee theft, minor frauds, and traffic violations committed and regulated informally within the community (unless they remain undetected altogether), the mass media present capital crimes (for example, murder, kidnapping, bank robbery) in a sensational and dramatized fashion. Immediately experienced crime differs in so many ways from the crime presented in the mass media that the actual experience of crime is very often not even perceived and recognized as such. In Western industrialized societies, 95 percent of all people gather their "experience" with violent crime, which they consider "real" crime, from the mass media, which they consider a reliable source of information (Garofalo, 1981:334; O'Connor, 1978). Television is perceived as the most trustworthy form of media, because it leaves its viewers under the impression of being immediately involved in a situation and of experiencing contemporary events with their own eyes. Yet, even live programs deliver, through picture selection and camera angles, mere interpretations rather than complete pictures of reality. An audience poll of the West German TV news programs *"Tagesschau"* ("Eyewitness News") and *"Heute"* ("Today") showed that 76 percent of their viewers considered these programs to be reliable (Abend, 1974: 174–75). In the United States, 80 percent of the interviewees delivered the opinion that the actual problem of crime was just as or even more serious than its portrayal in the mass media (Hindelang, Gottfredson, and Garofalo, 1978:172). These results show that public opinion is highly perceptive to the portrayal of crime in the mass media.

Public Opinion about Crime

Publicized opinion and public opinion on crime and criminal justice interact constantly. If one tries to gain an insight into the subjective state of public security on the basis of victimization surveys (Australian Bureau of Statistics, 1975, 1984; U.S. Department of Justice, 1983, 1984; Canadian Solicitor General, 1983–1985; Biles, 1985; Dijk and Steinmetz, 1980; Hough and Mayhew, 1983; Ishii, 1979; Fujimoto, 1982; Sveri, 1982; Manzanera, 1984; Clinard, 1978; Schwind et al., 1975; Stephan, 1976), one finds attitudes corresponding to those distributed by the mass media.

First, violent crimes and crimes against the person are considered to be the main criminal problems. Victimization surveys in numerous countries unanimously revealed that the importance of crime is perceived as being more extensive, serious, and threatening as frames of reference move further away from the respondent (see, for example, Hindelang et al., 1978:161; Stephan, 1976: 326). Criminality is seen to be increasing "somewhere else" but not in the immediate residential area. Outsiders, foreigners, and unknown offenders are held to be mainly responsible for the criminality that is inflicted upon the neighborhood, the society is victimized from the outside by an out-group. With the help of this projection, which was first discovered by psychoanalysis, the law-abiding citizen is able to transfer his criminal wishes into a social out-group, the criminals. The "we-they" dichotomy permits the socially conforming citizen to condemn more harshly the "abnormal," "psychopathic" offenders.

In contrast to this, delinquency and criminality, according to concurrent criminological research, are not distributed in the population as "either-or" but rather as "more or less" (see, for example, Erickson and Empey, 1963). Criminality is a continuum at the one end of which there are those offenders who commit many and serious crimes and who are discovered comparatively often, and at the other end of which are people who rarely commit petty crimes and whose criminality is mostly hidden and undiscovered. The transitions are fluid. This criminological model of the distribution of criminality, which is based on modern empirical criminological research, has not yet been adopted by the mass media. It is doubtful whether it will ever be accepted by them as it makes the societal projection and thus the recipients' experience of relief impossible.

Second, fear of crime has freed itself from its rational basis and concentrates predominantly on violent crimes committed by strangers. Since this type of crime is a very rare phenomenon, what the population fears is actually the least frequent of all law violations. Fear of sexual and violent crimes within the family or the community (for example, relatives, friends, acquaintances, neighbors) is less present in the population. These crimes are committed more frequently but remain to a large extent hidden and undetected, because they are not reported to the police. Neither is the population very worried about falling victim to traffic violations or to property and economic crimes, although these crimes are very widespread. Property and economic crimes, after all, have in most cases collective or anonymous, impersonal victims. Traffic violations are to a large extent considered pardonable offenses. Violent crimes committed by strangers are feared most by women and elderly people, although these sex and age groups are victimized less often than the population average (Braithwaite, Biles, and Whitrod, 1982; Brillon, 1983; Baril, 1983). Thus, fear of crime in women and elderly people has no basis in their actual victimization risks.

Third, the majority of the general population in Western industrialized societies believes that crime should be controlled on the one hand by reinforcement of the police in terms of increasing manpower and improving equipment and training, on the other hand by more severe sanctioning, sentencing, and execution of punishment (see, for example, Reiss, 1967; Teske and Farrar, 1978). Police performance is generally considered satisfactory. The general public overrates the importance of formal social control, of police, courts, and correctional institutions in the control of crime. The importance of informal social control in the prevention and control of delinquency through family, schools, and professional and recreational peer groups is largely underestimated. Informal social control, which works toward law-abiding, socially conforming behavior in a lifelong process of socialization, thereby supporting formal social control, must not, however, be confused with self-help that attempts to take the place of formal social control.

Consequences of Subjective States of Public Security in Reality

The constant interaction of publicized opinion and public opinion on crime and criminal justice has serious consequences in reality. As the reality of crime investigated through criminological research has almost no impact on the portrayal of crime in the mass media, the subjective state of public security loses its basis in reality. Although it is not the mass media alone who—through their unrealistic portrayal of criminality—produce fear of crime, aggressive life-styles, and an unjustified alteration of legislation and application of penal law (Harding, 1984), they form an important factor in the development of these socially damaging appearances. Their contribution to the rise of these phenomena is not inconsiderable, as a number of examples show.

Unlike those who watch little TV, the heavy viewer perceives the world as much more dangerous than it really is (Gerbner and Gross, 1976a, 1976b; Gordon and Heath, 1981). He is more distrustful and fearful than the light viewer. He considers himself to be in danger of criminal victimization. He lives in an exaggerated fear of crime, by which he feels threatened and toward which he assumes an insecure, emotional position. Here, the emotional fear of crime is caused not only through the form of the portrayal of crime, the dramatization and sensationalization of offenses, but the contents of the crime portrayal are highly important. An empirical criminological psychological study performed in Würzburg/Bavaria concludes that the reactions to offense and offender become more emotional, more fearful, less competent, and less *realistic* as the media portrays the offender's social and personal characteristics less rationally.

The portrayal of suicides on television leads to an increased number of suicides by teenagers. In the United States, the effects of thirty-eight nationally televised news or feature stories about suicide from 1973 to 1979 were investigated. A significant increase in suicides by teenagers within seven days after the television broadcasts was found (Phillips and Carstensen, 1986). These research results were confirmed by further empirical research carried out in New York in 1984–85 (Gould and Schaffer, 1986) and in the Federal Republic of Germany from 1981 to 1985 (Schmidtke and Haefner, 1986). The increase in suicides, which, in the Federal Republic of Germany, for the presented age group and for the presented kind of suicide, amounted to 167 percent and 175 percent, can only be explained by learning through observation of models (see also Wynn and Vinson, 1982).

Through a long-term study covering more than thirty years, it has been demonstrated (Eron and Huesmann, 1980, 1984) that continued viewing by children of violence on television exercises a lasting negative effect on the whole course of these children's lives and that it can lead to violent and criminal behavior in their adolescence and adulthood. Further empirical-psychological studies support this research result (Singer and Singer, 1980; Belson, 1978; but cf. Edgar, 1977; Gunter, 1985). Television teaches its audience aggressive styles of behavior. Through exposure to the perpetual repetition of media violence, the television audience not only becomes used to reacting aggressively if provoking circumstances seem to require such a behavior (Bandura, 1973), but the continual repetition of violence on the television screen also causes a reduction of emotional responsiveness to violence and a growing acceptance of aggressive attitudes and values (Goranson, 1970). Violence in the media results in satiation, habituation, and accommodation to aggression, which leads to a continual decline and finally to a disappearance of emotions. The perpetual presentation of violence on television creates a climate of aggression in society (Semmler, 1975).

Aggressive pornography causes a violent attitude toward women (Malamuth, 1984; Donnerstein, 1984). The suffering, the pain, the physical and mental damage of rape victims are not shown in pornographic films and videos. Through a "beautified," "illusionary" portrayal of sexual violence—for example through an involuntary orgasm of the rape victim—victims can pretend that the victim of rape enjoys the rape. Such aggressive pornography justifies the use of violence. Men and women learn, through models, the social prejudice toward "pleasant," sexually exciting, aggressive behavior (Nelson, 1982:203, 207). Men no longer have a negative attitude toward rape after they have watched aggressive-pornographic films and videos regularly; they become used to rape; they develop an aggressive attitude towards women.

Juvenile delinquency, as a general rule, does not arouse great interest in the mass media. An exception, however, is the delinquency of youth gangs. By the varying frequency of their reporting of delinquent activities of youth gangs, the mass media create the erroneous impression that the amount of youth-gang delinquency rises or falls, or that its distribution varies considerably in different big cities (Miller, 1976:95, 97, 105). The reaction of the mass media to gang delinquency satisfies the gang members' craving for recognition, and it supports the youth gang's bonds by producing a "moral panic" in the population and by creating "folk devils" (Cohen, 1980). The more infuriated the public is about gang delinquency, the more closely the youth gangs join up. Media reporting about gang delinquency fascinates other boys' groups and has contagious effects; public opinion is shaped and reinforced by the dramatic stereotypes of gang structures and activities.

Gang research has shown that media reports about gang delinquency have an effect on the gang members similar to the effect that theater reviews have on actors or sport reports have on professional soccer players. A gang receiving extensive news coverage is happily excited, since its reputation has been supported. Gangs that are not reported about are disappointed. As sensation and drama are well received in the mass media, the gangs try to act as sensationally and dramatically as possible (Miller, 1970:59, 61). They hope for additional publicity through spectacular violations of the law, to which they are spurred on by media reports. At the same time, through the public branding that occurs, gang members see themselves confirmed as delinquents, and they alter their personal identities increasingly towards delinquent personalities.

By the selection of special crime problems as subjects and by one-sided direction of public awareness, the mass media cause aggravations of penal laws and of their application that do not appear justified criminologically. This negative influence of the mass media was demonstrated long ago by Sutherland's (1950) research on the Criminal-Sexual Psychopath Laws, and by Becker's research on the Marijuana Tax Act with its penal provisions (1963: 135–46). A more recent example is the media coverage of the delinquency of Maori and Polynesian youth gangs in Auckland, New Zealand, in the years 1978 to 1980 (Kelsey and Young, 1982): gang activities were exaggerated in the mass media and presented as an oppressing social problem. As a result of these media dramatizations, two sections of the penal code were toughened and more severe sentences were imposed upon gang members. Increased police manpower and resources were made available, and the fear of gang delinquency rose in the population. The economic crisis of the mid-1970s, unemployment, and inflation had saturated the climate of opinion with a general fear of the future, which the mass media directed against the youth gangs, thus concretizing this fear. The youth gangs were socially visible, well organized, and their life-style, behavior, and values were completely contrary to those of the majority of the population. They were depicted as a novel threat to society, even though they had been a continuous problem. The social problem of economic crisis was turned into a personal problem of Maoris and Polynesians, who actually suffered most from unemployment.

Objections against the Submitted Concept

At the beginning of this paper it was hypothesized that criminological research results have virtually no influence on the portrayal of crime in the mass media and that the permanent unrealistic interaction between publicized opinion and public opinion has negative consequences in reality for the development of fear of crime, an aggressive life-style, and unjustified alterations of legislation and application of penal laws. Three objections to this hypothesis may be expressed.

The Influence Has Not Been Proved

The mass media and some social scientists (see, for example, Kerner and Feltes, 1980; Killias, 1983; Feltes and Ostermann, 1985) maintain that the influence of the mass media on the feelings, attitudes, and behavior of their audiences has not been proved, that it could not be proved at all. They plead that the operating mechanisms between mass media and audiences are very complex, that therefore linear causal links cannot be established and that the influence of the mass media cannot be separated from other factors of influence. This argument has the sympathy of the public, most of whom consider it degrading to be substantially influenced by the mass media in their feelings, attitudes, and behavior. They are too proud of their critical judgement ability to be influenced by the mass media in any respect. They do not—uncritical toward themselves as they are—try to account for the influences of the mass media.

The methodological difficulties of mass-media-influence research are not denied at all, though there is detailed psychological research that proves the effects of the mass media on their recipients. It seems wondrous, however, that the mass media deny their own influence. After all, they finance themselves mostly through advertising, and that trade and industry spends a lot of money for commercials in the mass media which—allegedly—exercise no influence on the public. It is furthermore surprising that the mass media, which—as is generally conceded—present reality-distorting violent crime portrayals, do not have to prove that their behavior is harmless; they lay the burden of proof on the social scientists who have already proved that the contents of the media are violent and reality-distorting.

Mass Media Do Not Create Fear of Crime

A North American study (Skogan and Maxfield, 1981) and a Swiss study (Killias, 1983) deny that the mass media create fear of crime. They do concede that violent crimes are rare phenomena in reality, that the mass media present violent criminality constantly and excessively, and that the emotional fear of crime in the population is very widespread. Still, they deny the part the mass media play in the causation of emotional fear of crime. This fear is held to develop only through personal victimization, through physical and social vulnerability to criminal victimization, and through personal conversations about crime. The advocates of this opinion are not able to explain the contradictions arising from the results of their studies. It is inexplicable why, on the one hand, victimization through violent crimes is rare, but, on the other hand, allegedly many people should know and talk to victims of violent crimes about their criminal victimization. Our victimological experience shows that, on the contrary, victims of violent crimes avoid talking about their victimization experiences. Furthermore, it is not plausible that personal conversations about crime should be based exclusively on actual victimization experiences, but not on the media portrayal of crimes.

Violence on TV Has no Effect on Behavior

A recent study carried out by a research team of the National Broadcasting Company (NBC), one of the three big commercial television networks in the United States (Milavsky et al., 1982), comes to the conclusion that the portrayal of violence on television has no effect whatsoever on the attitudes and styles of behavior of the television audience. This study, which wants to attribute violent behavior exclusively to the influences of the family and the neighborhood, is, however, not convincing. This is because it cannot provide reasons why aggressive learning models in the family and the neighborhood do affect the behavior, and learning models of television do not.

Recommendations for Criminologically Desirable Opinion Formation through the Mass Media

It is out of the question that the freedom of the press should be restricted in any way simply because research demonstrates negative consequences. However, media communicators cannot hide behind the assertion that the mass media have to entertain their recipients exclusively with crime and deviant behavior. In a democratic constitutional state of Western orientation, the mass media have to provide information about criminality and criminal justice, but preferably in an objective way. The media must instruct potential victims of crimes about their risks of victimization, they must control penal legislation and the criminal justice as "watchdogs of the public," and they must explain to society where the borderline is drawn between allowed and forbidden behavior (borderline hypothesis) (Erikson, 1966; Sturma, 1984). The mass media are by no means allowed to do as they please in the fulfilment of their tasks. They must not tolerate hate propaganda (Canadian Law Reform Commission, 1986), which, for example, during the time of National Socialism in Germany led to disastrous consequences.

The mass media cannot be made scapegoats, who alone are responsible for social deviance and crime. Although the present state of criminological media research suggests that the mass media contribute to the causation of crime, this does not mean that criminological research in the relationship between mass media and criminality has come to an end. The internal pressures within the mass media organizations that lead to the distortions in crime coverage must, on the contrary, be investigated in detail. Paul Wilson and Peter Grabovsky of the Australian Institute of Criminology in Canberra are presently conducting such a criminological research work. To my mind the media communicators, in their portrayals of crime, follow public opinion (interaction between publicized opinion and public opinion) about crime and criminal justice, rather than their personal beliefs. It is of great international interest which research outcome the Australian Institute of Criminology will achieve.

A realistic assessment of the present state seems to prohibit completely withdrawing the popular entertainment forms dealing with deviant and criminal fantasies from the public. However, the entertainment forms about criminality should not deviate as extremely from reality as is presently the case. Most of all, the mass media should in their entertainment forms on criminality not try to create the appearance of a criminal reality which does not correspond to fact. Rather, truthfulness should demand that they point out, in a suitable way, that television stories about crime are games, brain teasers, or modern fairy tales (Jung 1985a, 1985b).

The crime reports in the mass media have to convey to their audiences a more complete and more reality-oriented portrait of criminality, offenders, and victims. Crime news has to be completed through background information and through documentaries, which should be broadcast at prime time with a high audience rating and which should make the research results of criminology and their practical consequences understandable to a mass audience. It is not sufficient to quote criminologists; journalists have to acquaint themselves with the research results. It is not enough to hastily put together documentaries under the compulsion of actuality. The analysis of crime requires calmness, thoughtfulness, and patience. The journalist must have the courage to face the everyday occurrence and normality of crime. This, however, will be hard to do as the audiences are oversophisticated and spoiled by crime entertainment. But it is not impossible to achieve this if journalists can free themselves from the idea that their audiences want to see criminality in the way it is presently portrayed.

Above all, it is necessary that a larger public and especially the mass media be acquainted with the empirical research results of criminology in an understandable and modern fashion. The Australian Institute of Criminology performs pioneering work for world criminology in this respect by having issued the series Trends and Issues in Crime and Criminal Justice since 1986. The problem lies in a better cooperation between criminology and the mass media, to which both sides must contribute. Everything which is demanded here from the mass media can be summed up in one sentence: they should contribute to peace, truthfulness, and honesty so that in the future we can cope better with the problems of social deviance, juvenile delinquency, and criminality.

References

Abend, Michael. 1974. "Die Tagesschau: Zielvorstellungen und Produktionsbedingungen." *Rundfunk und Fernsehen* 22:166–87.

Adams, Phillip. 1975. "Films, Literature, and Crimes of Violence." *Australian Journal of Forensic Sciences* 7:149–56.

Australian Bureau of Statistics. 1975. *General Social Survey Crime Victims of May 1975*. Canberra.

———. *Crime Victims Survey, 1983, Preliminary*. Canberra.

Bandura, Albert. 1973. *Aggression. A Social Learning Analysis*. Englewood Cliffs, N.J.: Prentice-Hall.

———. 1977. *Social Learning Theory*. Englewood Cliffs, N.J.: Prentice-Hall.

Baril, Micheline. 1983. "Une Illustration de la Peur Concrète: Le Cas des Victimes." *Criminologie* 16:31–49.

Becker, Howard S. 1963. *Outsiders*. New York-London: Free Press–Collier-Macmillan.

Belson, William A. 1978. *Television Violence and the Adolescent Boy*. Westmead-Farnborough-Hampshire: Saxon House.

Biles, David. 1985. *Australian Victim Survey Methodology*. Lecture to the American Society of Criminology, San Diego.

Blumer, Herbert. 1972. "Society as Symbolic Interaction." In *Symbolic Interaction*. 2nd ed., edited by Jerome G. Manis and Bernard N. Meltzer. Boston: Allyn and Bacon.

Braithwaite, John, David Biles, and Ray Whitrod. 1982. "Fear of Crime in Australia." In *The Victim in International Perspective*, edited by Hans Joachim Schneider, pp. 220–28. Berlin-New York: Walter de Gruyter.

Brillon, Yves. 1983. "La Peur du Crime et la Punitivité chez les Personnes Agées." *Criminologie* 16:7–29.

Canadian Law Reform Commission. 1986. *Hate Propaganda*. Ottawa.

Canadian Solicitor General 1983–1985. *Canadian Urban Victimization Survey*. Six bulletins. Ottawa.

Chibnall, Steve. 1977. *Law-and-Order News. An Analysis of Crime Reporting in the British Press*. London: Tavistock.

Clinard, Marshall B. 1978. *Cities with Little Crime. The Case of Switzerland*. Cambridge-London-New York-Melbourne: Cambridge University Press.

Cohen, Stanley. 1980. *Folk Devils and Moral Panics. The Creation of the Mods and Rockers*. New York: St. Martin's Press.

Davis, F. James. 1952. "Crime News in Colorado Newspapers." In *The Manufacture of News*, edited by Stanley Cohen and Jack Young, pp. 127–35. London: Constable.

Dijk, Jan J. M. van. 1979. "The Extent of Public Information and the Nature of Public Attitudes towards Crime." In *Collected Studies in Criminological Research, vol. 17: "Public Opinion on Crime and Criminal Justice,"* edited by the Council of Europe, pp. 7–42. Strasbourg.

Dijk, Jan J. M. van, and Carl H. D. Steinmetz. 1980. *The Research and Documentation Centre Victim Surveys, 1974–1979*. The Hague.

Dominick, Joseph R., "Crime and Law Enforcement on Prime Time Television." *Public Opinion Quarterly* 37:241–50.

———. 1978. "Crime and Law Enforcement in the Mass Media." In *Deviance and the Mass Media*, edited by Charles Winick, pp. 105–28. Beverly Hills-London: Sage.

Donnerstein, Edward. 1984. "Pornography: Its Effect on Violence against Women." In *Pornography and Sexual Aggression*, edited by Neil M. Malamuth and Edward Donnerstein, pp. 53–81. New York-London-Tokyo: Academic Press.

Edgar, Patricia. 1977. *Children and Screen Violence*. St. Lucia, Queensland: University of Queensland Press.

Erickson, Maynard L., and LaMar T. Empey. 1963. "Court Records, Undetected Delinquency, and Decision-Making." *Journal of Criminal Law, Criminology, and Police Science* 54:456–69.

Erikson, Kai T. 1966. *Wayward Puritans*. New York-London-Sydney: John Wiley.

Eron, Leonard D., and L. Rowell Huesmann. 1980. "Adolescent Aggression and Television." In *Forensic Psychology and Psychiatry*, edited by Fred Wright, Charles Bahn, and Robert W. Rieber, pp. 319–31. New York: New York Academy of Sciences.

Feltes, Thomas, and Christian Ostermann. 1985. "Kriminalberichterstattung, Verbrechensfurcht und Stigmatisierung: Anmerkungen zu den (Unterstellten) Folgen von massenmedialen Verbrechensdarstellungen für Täter, Opfer und Bevölkerung." *Monatsschrift für Kriminologie und Strafrechtsreform* 68:261–68.

Fishman, Mark. 1978. "Crime Waves as Ideology." *Social Problems* 25:531–43.

Förster, Michael, and Josef Schenk. 1984. "Der Einfluß massenmedialer Verbrechensdarstellungen auf Verbrechensfurcht und Einstellungen zu Straftätern." *Monatsschrift für Kriminologie und Strafrechtsreform* 67:90–104.

Fujimoto, Tetsuya. 1982. "The Victimological Study in Japan." In *The Victim in International Perspective*, edited by Hans Joachim Schneider, pp. 128–50. Berlin-New York: Walter de Gruyter.

Garofalo, James. 1981. "Crime and the Mass Media: A Selective Review of Research." *Journal of Research in Crime and Delinquency* 18:319–50.

Geerds, Friedrich. 1979. "Fahndung im Fernsehen. Kriminalistische und kriminologische Aspekte." In *Fahndungssendungen im Fernsehen,* edited by Burkhard Hirsch, Gerhard Weis, Ernst Fuehr, and Friedrich Geerds, pp. 42–72. München: Beck.

Gerald, J. Edward. 1983. *News of Crime.* Westport, Conn.-London: Greenwood.

Gerbner, George, and Larry P. Gross. 1976a. "Living with Television: The Violence Profile." *Journal of Communication* 26:173–99.

———. 1976b. "The Scary World of TV's Heavy Viewer." *Psychology Today* 4:41–45.

Goranson, Richard E. 1970. "Media Violence and Aggressive Behavior: A Review of Experimental Research." In *Advances in Experimental Social Psychology,* vol. 5, edited by Leonard Berkowitz. New York-London: Academic Press.

Gordon, Margaret T., and Linda Heath. 1981. "The News Business, Crime, and Fear." In *Reactions to Crime,* edited by Dan A. Lewis, pp. 227–50. Beverly Hills-London: Sage.

Gould, Madelyn S., and David Schaffer. 1986. "The Impact of Suicide in Television Movies." *New England Journal of Medicine* 315:690–94.

Graber, Dorris A. 1980. *Crime and the Public.* New York: Praeger.

Gunter, Barrie. 1985. *Dimensions of Television Violence.* Aldershot: Gower.

Harding, Richard W. 1984. *The Impact of Mass Media upon Youth Violence.* Beijing, China.

Hess, Albert G., and Dorothy A. Mariner. 1975. "On the Sociology of Crime Cartoons." *International Journal of Criminology and Penology* 3:253–65.

Hindelang, Michael J., Michael R. Gottfredson, and James Garofalo. 1978. *Victims of Personal Crime: An Empirical Foundation for a Theory of Personal Victimization.* Cambridge, Mass.: Ballinger.

Hoefnagels, G. Peter. 1973. *The Other Side of Criminology.* Deventer, Holland: Kluwer.

Höing, Rita. 1983. *Kriminalitätsdarstellung in den Fernsehnachrichten. Eine empirische Untersuchung der Sendungen "Tagesschau" und "Heute".* Münster: Phototechnische Zentralstelle.

Hough, Mike, and Pat Mayhew. 1983. *The British Crime Survey: First Report.* London: Her Majesty's Stationary Office.

Humphries, Drew. 1981. "Serious Crime, News Coverage, and Ideology. A Content Analysis of Crime Coverage in a Metropolitan Paper." *Crime and Delinquency* 27:191–205.

Ishii, Akira. 1979. "Die Opferbefragung in Tokyo." In *Das Verbrechensopfer*, edited by Gerd Ferdinand Kirchhoff and Klaus Sessar, pp. 133–57. Bochum: Norbert Brockmeyer.

Jones, E. Terrence. 1976. "The Press as Metropolitan Monitor." *Public Opinion Quarterly* 40:239–44.

Jubelius, Werner. 1981. *Darstellung der Instanzen sozialer Kontrolle.* Frankfurt, M.-Bern: Peter Lang.

———. 1984. "The Control of Aggressive Behavior by Changes in Attitudes, Values, and the Conditions of Learning." In *Advances in the Study of Aggression,* vol. 1, edited by Robert J. Blanchard and D. Caroline Blanchard, pp. 139–71. New York-London-Tokyo: Academic Press.

Jung, Heike. 1985a. "Massenmedien und Kriminalität." In *Kleines Kriminologisches Wörterbuch.* 2nd ed., edited by Günter Kaiser, Hans-Jürgen Kerner, Fritz Sack, and Hartmut Schellhoss, pp. 294–99. Heidelberg: C. F. Müller.

———. 1985b. "Was können die Medien in der kriminalpolitischen Meinungsbildung leisten?" In *Entwicklungslinien der Kriminologie,* edited by Gerhard Kielwein, pp. 47–57. Cologne-Berlin-Bonn-Munich: Carl Heymanns.

Kelsey, Jane, and Warren Young. 1982. *The Gangs: Moral Panic as Social Control.* Wellington: Victoria University.

Kerner, Hans-Jürgen. 1978. "Fear of Crime and Attitudes towards Crime. Comparative Criminological Reflections." *Annales Internationales de Criminologie* 17:83–99.

———. 1980. *Kriminalitätseinschätzung und Innere Sicherheit.* Wiesbaden: Bundeskriminalamt.

Kerner, Hans-Jürgen, and Thomas Feltes. 1980. "Medien, Kriminalitätsbild und Offentlichkeit. Einsichten und Probleme am Beispiel einer Analyse von Tageszeitungen." In *Strafvollzug und Offentlichkeit,* edited by Helmut Kury, pp. 73–112. Freiburg i.Br.: Rombach.

Killias, Martin. 1982. "Zum Einfluß der Massenmedien auf Wissen und Meinung über Tötungsdelikte." *Monatsschrift für Kriminologie und Strafrechtsreform* 65:18–29.

———. 1983. "Massenmedien und Kriminalitätsfurcht: Abschied von einer plausiblen Hypothese." *Schweizerische Zeitschrift für Soziologie* 2:419–36.

Malamuth, Neil M. 1984. "Aggression against Women: Cultural and Individual Causes." In *Pornography and Sexual Aggression,* edited by Neil M. Malamuth and Edward Donnerstein, pp. 19–52. New York-London-Tokyo: Academic Press.

Manzanera, Luis Rodriguez. 1984. "Victimization in a Mexican City." In

Victimization and Fear of Crime: World Perspectives, U.S. Department of Justice, Bureau of Justice Statistics, pp. 51–56. Washington D.C.: Superintendent of Documents, U.S. Government Printing Office.

Mattern, Ulrich. 1983. "Massenmedien und Kriminalität." In *Kriminal- und Rechtspsychologie*, edited by Willi Seitz, pp. 120–28. Munich-Vienna-Baltimore: Urban and Schwarzenberg.

Mead, George Herbert. 1976. *Sozialpsychologie*. Darmstadt: Wissen-schaftliche Buchgesellschaft.

Milavsky, J. Ronald, Ronald C. Kessler, Horst H. Stipp, and William S. Rubens. 1982. *Television and Aggression*. New York-London: Academic Press.

Miller, Walter B. 1970. "White Gangs." In *Modern Criminals*, edited by James F. Short, pp. 45–85. Chicago: Aldine.

———. 1976. "Youth Gangs in the Urban Crisis Era." In *Delinquency, Crime, and Society*, edited by James F. Short, pp. 91–128. Chicago-London: University of Chicago Press.

Nelson, Edward C. 1982. "Pornography and Sexual Aggression." In *The Influence of Pornography on Behavior*, edited by Maurice Yaffé and Edward C. Nelson, pp. 177–248. Paris-San Francisco-Tokyo: Academic Press.

O'Connor, Michael. 1978. "A Community's Opinion on Crime: Some Preliminary Findings." *Australian and New Zealand Journal of Sociology* 14:61–64.

Ostermeyer, Helmut. 1971. "Straflust statt Rechtsbewußtsein." In *Die Tabus der bundesdeutschen Presse*, edited by Eckart Spoo, pp. 82–96. Munich-Vienna: Carl Hanser.

———. 1975. *Die bestrafte Gesellschaft*. Munich-Vienna: Carl Hanser.

Pandiani, John A. 1978. "Crime TV: If All We Knew Is What We Saw." *Contemporary Crises* 2:437–58.

Phillips, David P., and Lundic L. Carstensen. 1986. "Clustering of Teenage Suicides after Television News Stories about Suicide." *New England Journal of Medicine* 315:685–89.

Reiss, Albert J. 1967. *Public Perceptions and Recollections about Crime, Law Enforcement, and Criminal Justice*. Washington D.C.: Superintendent of Documents, U.S. Government Printing Office.

Reiwald, Paul. 1948. *Die Gesellschaft und ihre Verbrecher*. Zurich: Pan.

Riklin, Franz. 1981. "Stigmatisierungsproblematik und Tätigkeit der Medien im Rahmen der Strafverfolgung und der Prozeßberichterstattung." In *Stigmatisierung durch Strafverfahren und Strafvollzug*, edited by Walter T. Haesler, pp. 129–59. Diessenhofen: Rüegger.

Roshier, Bob. 1973. "The Selection of Crime News by the Press." In *The Manufacture of News*, edited by Stanley Cohen and Jock Young, pp. 28–39. London: Constable.

Schima, Konrad. n.d. "Kriminologische Aspekte der Fahndung im Fernsehen." In *Kriminalität, Brutalität und dargestellte Aggression im Fernsehen und ihre Wirkung auf die Öffentlichkeit*, edited by Österreichischer Rundfunk, pp. 367–94. Vienna.

Schmidtke, Armin, and Heinz Haefner. 1986. "Die Vermittlung von Selbstmordmotivation und Selbstmordhandlung durch fiktive Modelle." *Nervenarzt* 57:502–10.

Schneider, Hans Joachim. 1977. *Kriminalitätsdarstellung im Fernsehen und kriminelle Wirklichkeit*. Opladen: Westdeutscher Verlag.

———. 1979a. "Massenmedien." In *Handwörterbuch der Kriminologie*. 2nd edition, vol. IV edited by Rudolf Sieverts and Hans Joachim Schneider Berlin-New York: Walter de Gruyter 1979a, 338–393.

———. 1979b. "The Influence of Mass Communication Media on Public Opinion on Crime and Criminal Justice." In *Collected Studies in Criminological Research*. vol. 17: *Public Opinion on Crime and Criminal Justice*, edited by Council of Europe, pp. 121–60. Strasbourg.

———. 1980. *Das Geschäft mit dem Verbrechen. Massenmedien und Kriminalität*. Munich: Kindler.

———. 1981. "Massenmedien und Kriminalität." In *Die Psychologie des 20. Jahrhunderts*. vol. 14: *Auswirkungen auf die Kriminologie*, edited by Hans Joachim Schneider, pp. 631–82. Zurich: Kindler.

———. 1982. "Meinungsbildung durch den Rundfunk über Straftaten und deren Ahndung." In *Meinungsbildung durch den Rundfunk über Straftaten und deren Ahndung*, edited by Dietrich Oehler, Inge Donnepp, Hubert Rohde, Hans Joachim Schneider, and L. Kos-Rabcewicz-Zubkowski, pp. 41–68.

———. 1987. *Kriminologie*. Berlin-New York: Walter de Gruyter.

Schwacke, Bettina. 1983. *Kriminalitätsdarstellung in der Presse*. Frankfurt/M.-Bern-New York: Peter Lang.

Schwind, Hans-Dieter, Wilfried Ahlborn, Hans Jürgen Eger, Ulrich Jany, Volker Pudel, and Rüdiger Weiß. 1975. *Dunkelfeldforschung in Göttingen 1973/74*. Wiesbaden: Bundeskriminalamt.

Semmler, Clement. 1975. "Mass Media: Literature and Crimes of Violence." *Australian Journal of Forensic Sciences* 7:135–48.

Sherizen, Sanford. 1978. "Social Creation of Crime News. In *Deviance and the Mass Media*, edited by Charles Winick, pp. 203–24. Beverly Hills-London: Sage.

Singer, Dorothy G., and Jerome L. Singer. 1980. "Television Viewing and Aggressive Behavior in Preschool Children: A Field Study." In *Forensic Psychology and Psychiatry*, edited by Fred Wright, Charles Bahn, and Robert W. Rieber, pp. 289–303. New York: New York Academy of Sciences.

Skogan, Wesley G. 1981. "On Attitudes and Behaviors." In *Reactions to Crime,* edited by Dan A. Lewis, pp. 19–45. Beverly Hills-London: Sage.

Skogan, Wesley G., and Michael G. Maxfield. 1981. *Coping with Crime.* Beverly Hills-London: Sage.

Stein-Hilbers, Maria Helene. 1976. *Kommunikation über Verbrechen. Empirische Untersuchung der Darstellung von Kriminalität im Fernsehen.* Munich: Schön.

Stephan, Egon. 1976. *Die Stuttgarter Opferbefragung.* Wiesbaden: Bundeskriminalamt.

Sturma, Michael. 1984. "Crime News in Colonial New South Wales." *Media Information Australia* 7–13.

Sutherland, Edwin H. 1950. "The Diffusion of Sexual Psychopath Laws." In *Crime and Justice in Society,* edited by R. Quinney, 1969, pp. 88–97. Boston: Little, Brown and Company.

Sveri, Knut. 1982. "Comparative Analyses of Crime by Means of Victim Surveys. The Scandinavian Experience." In *The Victim in International Perspective,* edited by Hans Joachim Schneider, pp. 209–19. Berlin-New York: Walter de Gruyter.

Teske, Raymond H. C., and Greg P. Farrar. 1978. *Texas Crime Poll.* Huntsville: Sam Houston State University.

U.S. Department of Justice, Bureau of Justice Statistics. 1984. *Criminal Victimization in the United States, 1981, 1982.* Washington D.C.: Superintendent of Documents, U.S. Government Printing Office.

Wisehart, M. K. 1922. "Newspapers and Criminal Justice." In *Criminal Justice in Cleveland,* edited by Roscoe Pound and Felix Frankfurter. Reprint: Montclair, N.J.: Patterson Smith.

Wynn, P. W., and T. Vinson. 1982. "The Media as a Cause of Crime and Fear." In *National Symposium on Victimology,* edited by Peter N. Graborsky, pp. 183–94. Canberra: Australian Institute of Criminology.

7

Epistemological Problems in Criminology

Alexander Yakovlev

Criminology as a science occupies a rather peculiar position among the social sciences. Trying to synthesize sociology and law, it is called upon to provide objective descriptions of crimes and their related phenomena. It is expected to explain them, to predict future tendencies, and to recommend how to regulate reality in a socially acceptable direction.

The object of criminological study is something that is considered by the dominant law and morals as negative, dangerous, or harmful. Criminology must study, describe, and explain something that is considered extremely undesirable for a given society, something that reveals society's shortcomings and weaknesses. Under certain social conditions, something that is regarded as desirable and right collides with something that exists in fact. The collision between "is" and "ought" poses a dilemma: whether to direct theoretical thinking to the "positive" side of things, to describe that which is in accordance with declarations, pronouncements, etc., neglecting all that is in contradiction to them; or whether to direct critical analysis to the objective reality, irrespective of its content. In the first instance this collision is eliminated only in the theoretical imagination; in the second, there arises the possibility of overcoming this collision by means of a social reality transformation.

The outcome of this collision may be influenced by certain epistemological peculiarities. Criminology is supposed to be a science studying objective reality. The rules for finding the relevant facts, criteria for their selection, and methods for analyzing them—these are basic epistemological problems. The facts of life constitute an objective basis that is reflected by the facts of science. But what is the social reality? Which are these facts of life? They are constructed out of material objects and things, and out of ideal entities—moral prescriptions, norms, legal ideas, in short, such "things" as play a compelling role for individual behavior by way of restricting an individual's whims. The word "thing" is used here in quotation marks for good reason, because among them there are also, for example, generally accepted ethical-moral norms and moral imperatives, which regulate the everyday activities of people; legal institutions and various forms of the state—political organizations; and ritually legalized behavior patterns—the rules of life that are mandatory for a member of a given society.

Two important features characterize these "things," or social facts. First, they exist objectively as material objects and events. They are ideal entities, existing outside the consciousness of any particular individual. They exist quite objectively, independent from the consciousness and will of an individual. This is reality sui generis, unseen and untouchable. Side by side with the material facts (the material conditions of social life), there are social facts, which also determine an individual's behavior. Second, social facts are principally different from mere material facts, that is, "material" forms of social life. They are the facts of collective consciousness. They are the ideal essence of social life.

To ignore the essential difference between the material and social facts means to underestimate the specific nature of the latter. And ascribing to social facts the properties of material ones, that is, reduction of the social facts to material facts, leads to specific epistemological aberrations in criminological theory.

Reification

These aberrations express themselves first in the so-called reification of the social processes, phenomena, and categories, among them such categories as "crime," "criminality," and "criminal personality." As it was expressed by the Norwegian criminologist Nils Christie, "[C]rime is not a thing. Crime is a concept applicable in certain social situations where it is possible and in the interests of one or several parties to apply it" (1981:74). The American sociologist David Silverman says that "one of the traditional weaknesses of sociological analysis is the reification of human institutions, that is, to approach them on the common sense ground, considering them as facts, objects, things" (Filmer et al., 1987:294, 303). Indeed, regarding socially organized categories as "external" objects similar to physical objects is typical for everyday thinking. Reification of criminological categories leads to certain epistemological and sociopractical consequences. Reification means "transformation into a thing." (Of course, this transformation takes place not in reality but only in the mind of the thinking person.) Reification results in a tendency to interpret socially conditioned acts as if they had a "natural property" of their own and performed in a society on the basis of their own laws.

In criminology, the concept of reification expresses itself in the "natural crime" conception. It focuses on crimes that are "inherently" criminal. These deeds are considered unchangeable in their properties. Their "criminal qualities" are embodied in them, and this very quality, supposedly, may be objectively established, the same way as any property of any material object. And supposedly these "natural crimes" compose the kernel, the main body, of any given criminality. Regardless of the evident contradiction to historical reality, this supposition is still to be found and reflected in the works of some clinical criminologists.

On this basis one could, thus, easily endeavor to engage in criminological research for purposes of revealing and describing the concrete contours, boundaries, and outer limits of the criminality of a given society, as an objectively existing, qualitatively distinguishable sum of crimes localized in the concrete sphere of social space. One could equally study the personality of any criminal, to reveal and describe his specific criminal qualities and to ascribe these to a specific part of the body or the mind, to the criminal's personality structure, and thus look at criminals as a special, qualitatively different category or group (or breed or class) of people. As an example, we may refer to the theory depicting the lower class culture as generating the milieu of gang delinquency (Miller, 1958).

But this is where serious epistemological difficulties begin. Very soon it becomes clear that the very basis of criminological research—criminal statistics—differs in principle from, for example, meteorological statistics. At the root of this distinction lies the specificity of social facts, which makes them different from material ones. A crime becomes a fact when and only when (1) somewhere a certain change in social reality, a certain event takes place, and (2) this event is acknowledged and evaluated as a crime (a day above freezing, or one below freezing, is not in need of such evaluation).

A material fact becomes such at the very instant that a change takes place in the material world, the world of things.

A social fact becomes such only after an objective change in reality, when a certain event receives specific social attributes from the outside, from the social structure (group, class and, eventually, from the state and law). And only after thus acquiring its social nature does a given event become a fact of the social world.

For a fact or event to become a social fact, to acquire its social meaning and significance, this fact or event must be included in a system of social information, become a fact of social, collective consciousness, become a part of it and consequently acquire the capacity to influence this consciousness and to change it accordingly. Only by way of changing the social consciousness can a social fact influence the people's behavior in a specific area. On the other hand, something that did not enter the consciousness of the social community and did not enter public consciousness (something that is not known, not recognized and, therefore, not evaluated, that, thus, does not become an object of people's attention and of social reaction), in sum, something that was not included in the society's informational structure will not become a social fact and, therefore, will be inconsequential for people's behavior.

There arises a problem. This process of incorporating certain facts and events into the society's informational system depends upon the sociopolitical organization of society. The process of perception, cognition, and evaluation of these facts and events depends upon the dominant sociopsychological attitudes, opinions, stereotyped notions, etc. This process reflects them and serves as their projection.

Of course, a significant share in this process of social-facts construction is attributable to the legal definitions of criminality. These definitions are essentially a result of socially predetermined selection, a negative evaluation and sorting of specific instances out of the whole amount of relevant facts. As is very well known, the number of violent deaths is, as a rule, much greater than the number of legally recognized homicides or murders. An instance of violent death (material fact) may become (or may not become) a criminally punishable homicide (social fact).

Whether a material fact becomes a social fact, or whether a given event receives the status of crime, depends not only on the legal definition and prohibition, but, in reality, it also depends on the evaluation of this event by the persons who witness it, or who suffer from it. Sometimes there are situations when life is so saturated with crimes that they are regarded as something as inevitable as bad weather, and nobody seems to be bothered by or concerned with them. They may not even be reported to the police (Clark, 1975:57). Eventually a social evaluation of an event as a crime as defined by criminal law is neutralized practically at the really decisive point—in the sphere of real everyday life encounters. An event loses its social-fact quality, is reduced to the level of a natural event, exactly at the point of perception and evaluation of the event by the evaluators. If, for example, the law makes moonshining a crime, but the people largely ignore this norm of law, then the process of distilling alcohol remains just a material (chemical) fact. It may even receive a positive evaluation in direct contradiction to the norm of law. One and the same material fact may indeed be embodied in quite different (and even opposing) social facts. At the root of this situation lies the inevitable specificity of the social facts, namely that they embody in themselves, as an inseparable entity, the objectively existing event and its subjective evaluation.

If this specificity of social facts is ignored, there arises the possibility of equating an official criminal statistic with the real number of crimes. If criminality is understood as just a sum of truly "criminal" events of truly objective reality (as if they were material facts) the temptation arises to compute a crime rate unadjusted by the impact of other parts of the social structure. Thus, the mode of thinking based only on the mechanical manipulation of material objects proves inadequate for the solution of social problems.

Reification of social, moral-ethical problems leads very often to biological reductionism. Thus, in the term "social instinct," the category "instinct," which is purely biological in nature, reduces the category "social" to the level of the inborn properties of an individual. The criminological theory based on the XYY chromosome falls into this category.

Having considered some epistemological consequences of the underestimation of the essential specificity of social facts (the reification of the conception of crime), we now turn to a seemingly quite opposite approach to the problem of defining crime, an approach that leads to another epistemological aberration. This may be called the "deification" of social facts.

Deification

This epistemological aberration is not a mere accidental deviation. It arises out of real properties of the cognitive process, being a result of a certain overestimation, an exaggeration of the subjective side of social facts. Of course, the conception of crime is directly linked to the dominant ideas, shared values, stereotyped notions, and definitions of crime in law. In other words, the crime conception really and objectively exists in the world of ideas, but not in the world of things. In this connection, the possibility arises of "deifying" these concepts, by ascribing to them the role of independent creators of social reality.

As was shown above, a social fact cannot be regarded as identical with a material fact. But it must not be absolutely separated from the material fact, or counterposed to it. Deification of the sociocultural conceptions is linked to the idealistic point of view that regards so-called constitutive meanings (Fay, 1975:76, 78) as the basis for social practice, ascribing to them the role of creators of social reality, of social practice. In criminology, the deification of sociocultural conceptions (crime and criminality conceptions included) leads to an underestimation of the material conditions of social life, conditions which, in the final analysis, determine these conceptions and produce them in the course of social life.

In criminological theory, this kind of deification leads to ascribing the decisive role in crime conception to such objectified, definite, but ideal (in character) categories as morals, ethics, law, etc. Criminality, consequently, is seen as a phenomenon of the social, collective consciousness and as its projection and creation (*o tempora, o mores!*). The individual perpetrator's crime is seen exclusively as a product of his will, his consciousness, or (in psychoanalytical theory) as the result of a broken-down defense mechanism. In this way a crime is seen as a manifestation of an individual's psychology, and criminality is viewed as the sum total of these psychological phenomena.

The Dutch criminologist, Louk Hulsman, is right when he stresses the historically conditioned, relative character of crime conceptions, and when he refuses to regard crime and criminals as specific, qualitatively distinctive categories. He concludes that, if it is the law that says what is and what is not a crime, then it is precisely the law that creates the criminal (Hulsman and Celis, 1982:68). As mentioned earlier, it is right to say that any event, any material fact becomes a social fact (in our case—a crime) in so far (and only in so far) as this fact receives an estimation of its social meaning and significance from a social entity (in our case in the form of a definition in criminal law). Only in this sense does "law create a crime." But would it be right to conclude that if law "creates" crime, then all we have to do is repeal the law and crime will disappear?

It is true that the legal conception of crime may achieve a relatively independent existence over time, sometimes taking on the stability of a social stereotype. Law conception is indeed a reflection of the dominant values and ideas. But would it be right to say, as Hulsman does, that to abolish criminal justice means just to establish a new way of thinking that refuses to see as crime what existing criminal justice systems consider as crime? I think not. From my point of view this is a clear example of an epistemological aberration, namely a deification of the conception of crime.

Criminal law, with its crime conception serving as a basis for the criminal justice system, is but a part of the much broader sociolegal structure of society. The definition of crime is but a negative reflection of the dominant value system, reflected in the positive norms of law-abiding behavior. One set of norms is inseparable from another. The conception of theft is inseparable from the conception of property. Property, as a social institution, is mainly a reflection of the material conditions of life. It is connected with the dominant mode of production, the division of labor, etc. Law includes both the conception of property rights and the conception of theft. These conceptions are opposite in meaning and social function, but identical in regard to their source, namely the social construction of society. The one cannot disappear without the disappearance of the other. Violent crime also is not an isolated phenomenon created by a legal definition. Law includes the right of the state to exercise "legal" violent means, and to prohibit "illegal" violence. These conceptions are opposite in meaning and social function, but identical in regard to their source—the social construction of society. The one cannot disappear without the disappearance of the other. But the social construction of societies is dependent on the material conditions of social life, on material facts. These conditions determine the dominant interests which in their turn determine the essence of a given system of law.

Summary

By seeing the social facts as identical with the material ones, and ignoring the specificity of social facts, we are in danger of reifying the social facts, of ascribing to them the properties of things, of material objects. Wrenching away a social fact from its material source, abstracting this fact from its material basis, ascribing to the social fact the quality of an independent, self-producing phenomenon, we are in danger of deifying the social fact. These are some of the epistemological aberrations which may be encountered by criminologists. They may serve as a barrier to a penetrating, socially critical analysis in criminology. In the first case, the important role of society, of social class, of the state, are ignored in the

TABLE 7.1
Reification and Deification

| Criminological Conceptions | MODES OF THINKING | |
	Reification	Deification
Crime	Sum of "natural" crimes (natural-material phenomena)	Sum of value-laden conceptions, criminal law definitions (collective consciousness phenomena)
Criminal	Born criminal and his contemporary modifications (biological phenomena)	Free, evil will (individual consciousness phenomena)

process of crime definition. In the second case, we are ignoring the material facts in our criminological analysis, above productive relations. These material conditions are revealed simultaneously in actions that are dangerous for the dominant interests, as well as in actions and institutions (law, state, etc.) that define them as crimes.

These are the restrictions on the critical function of criminology, as a consequence of resorting to reification and deification in criminological theory. Schematically, they may be presented as in table 7.1.

References

Christie, Nils. 1981. *Limits to Pain*. Oslo: Universitetsforlaget.

Clark, Ramsey. 1975. *Crime in America* (in Russian). American edition. New York: Simon and Schuster, 1970.

Fay, Brian. 1975. *Social Theory and Political Practice*. Winchester, Mass.: Unwin Hyman.

Filmer, Paul, Michael Philipson, David Silverman, and David Walsh. 1987. *New Directions in Social Theory* (in Russian).

Hulsman, L. H. C., and J. Beroat de Celis. 1982. *Peines Perdues*. Paris.

Miller, Walter. 1958. "Lower Class Culture as a Generating Milieu of Gang Delinquency." *Journal of Social Issues* 14:267–77.

8

The State of Criminology: Theoretical Decay or Renaissance

John Braithwaite

Introduction

This chapter and the following, by Joan McCord, developed from a panel at the American Society of Criminology (ASC) meeting in Montreal. At that meeting, without prior discussion, John Braithwaite and Joan McCord addressed similar issues. The papers differed regarding positions on these issues. The editors of *Advances in Criminological Theory* suggested that we publish our views as a step toward opening wider debate. Our papers are printed here with only minor changes.

In chapter 9, McCord traverses a wider sweep of issues at the heart of the criminological enterprise. In this chapter, Braithwaite focuses more narrowly on the possibility of general theories of crime. On the question of definition, Braithwaite argues that crime is a useful category of analysis, while McCord counsels caution over definitional categories that are too encompassing; they agree that definition is important and value-laden in a way that crucially shapes the kind of scholarship produced.

McCord argues for the value of longitudinal studies and against a preoccupation with psychological hedonism in criminological microtheory. These issues were not addressed by Braithwaite. There is sharp disagreement on the desirability of a grand or general theory, which Braithwaite supports and McCord contests. The papers are presented in the order in which they appeared at the ASC meetings.

The State of Criminology: Theoretical Decay or Renaissance?

A starving English slum dweller notices the baker's shop is unattended, grabs a loaf of bread to feed his family, and is subsequently apprehended and transported to Australia as a convict.

A factory manager faces the choice between slowing down production to ensure that the company complies with environmental pollution laws or not worrying about the effluent and meeting her production target. She does not believe that the latter would be "criminal"; it would merely be a breach of an unreasonable standard imposed by an antibusiness government. It is late at night, a time when she knows there is no chance of a government inspector appearing on the scene, so she lets the effluent flow.

A young black man is jilted by his girlfriend; he is angry, bitter, impulsive; he suffered some brutalizing experiences in the Vietnam war where he participated in the sexual torture of a village woman; he ingests some alcohol; he sees a woman alone in a dark street; he rapes and viciously bashes her.

Every crime event has a unique and complex causal history; the foregoing are simplified causal histories. A myriad of additional causes might have been added to each causal history, and each of these would itself have many causes. These are also causes of the crime, and they in turn have their causes. Even as simplified causal histories, the nature of the causes and the nature of the crimes seem so different as to defy the possibility of a general theory of crime. The conventional criminological wisdom of recent decades seems well founded—crime is so disparate a category and individual differences among criminals so great that general explanations are fantasies.

Accepting this appearance has been, I will argue, a mistake for criminology. Even though crime events have quite different causal histories, it may still be that there are elements common to all, or most, without which crime would not have occurred. Disparate as the three illustrative causal histories are, at least one common causal element can be abstracted from all three—an illegitimate opportunity: the unattended loaf of bread, the chance to leak the effluent in the dead of night, the vulnerable woman on a dark street. Also we might abstract a blockage of legitimate opportunity from all three: the unavailability to the slum dweller of legitimate means of feeding his family, the blockage of legitimate means for the factory manager to achieve her production target, the denial of consensual sexual access to the rapist's girlfriend. Just as we can abstract common opportunity theory causes from these otherwise disparate causal histories, so we might abstract common differential association or social learning theory elements from all three. With all three, there may have been exposure to definitions favorable to crime: the father's social learning that feeding his family is a higher loyalty than loyalty to the criminal law, the factory manager's rationalizations that pollution is not real crime, the legitimation of sexual violence directed against women that the rapist had experienced in Vietnam.

In principle, a general theory of crime can be very powerful even though it ignores all but one of the myriad causes in the varied causal histories of crime events. If that one cause is present in all causal histories that lead to crime and absent in all those that do not, then we have explained 100 percent of the variance in crime with our single-factor theory. And massive individual differences in the propensity to offend and in the environmental contingencies confronted do not detract from this fact in the least. They do not detract from the fact that if we can change this factor, whatever else is going on, crime will not occur. And of course, to be useful, a general theory is not required to explain all of the variance in all types of cases, but some of the variance in all types of cases.

My first point is, therefore, that it is nonsense to suggest that, because the behavior subsumed under the crime rubric is so disparate and has such complexly different causal histories, general theories of crime are impossible. A theory of any topic X will be an implausible idea unless there is a prior assumption that X is an explanandary kind. To be an explanandary kind, X need not be fully homogeneous, only sufficiently homogeneous for it to be likely that every or most types of X will come under one or more of the same causal influences. There is no way of knowing that a class of actions is of an explanandary kind short of a plausible theory of the class being developed. In advance, giraffes, clover, and newts might seem a hopelessly heterogeneous class, yet the theory of evolution includes them as members of a class whose members have a common origin.

At this point, some may be willing to concede that a variable like availability of illegitimate opportunities will be a correlate of all types of crime, even though only a partial explanation because so many with illegitimate opportunities will decline to take them. Yet, they will remain pessimistic about a general theory because opportunity explanations or differential association explanations, while they might be general, are also banal. The challenge for theoretical criminology is to take such general, uncontroversial—banal if you will—explanations and give them the specificity of content that will ultimately build criminological theory into something that can supply the uninitiated with new insight into the explanation of crime. We should not walk away from the challenge because its foundations are banal; this very banality can give solidity to the foundations of the theoretical edifices we build.

Before moving on to a consideration of why criminology has failed to build sophisticated theories on the foundations of its banalities, I must deal more pointedly with what is most widely seen in the contemporary debate as the fundamental impediment to general positive theory. This is that the answer to the question "What is crime?" is problematic. Crime is socially defined through processes of situationally negotiating meanings from subjective interpretations of social action. The last thing I would want to do is deny this. Nor would I challenge the observation that what counts as a crime is historically contingent: the content of the criminal code is the product of social conflicts settled differently in different societies and at different points in time within the same society.

What we must challenge is any contention that such observations demonstrate the impossibility or incoherence of general criminological theory. The second of our causal histories of crime illustrated a factory manager who believed that her pollution offense was not really crime; rather it was a minor breach of an unreasonable regulation. Let us assume that the courts would be clear in judging her action as criminal. "What is crime?" was problematic for her, yet we saw that this created no particular difficulties in accounting for her action in the terms of opportunity or differential association theory.

What is a crime will always be contested by those accused of being criminals. Scholars who study the way offenders contest the social reality of crime must be wary of a dangerous kind of political partisanship. One can study the perceptions of convicted rapists—that what happened was seduction rather than rape, that the victim gave him the come on, that she had "frothy knickers" (Taylor, 1972), that she was his wife who had always liked such treatment before—and one can conclude from the persistent repetitions of such accounts that the crime is so ambiguous and contested as to be a useless category of analysis. One can study the perceptions of business executives and their legal advisers that breaches of environmental or occupational health-and-safety laws are not really crimes and conclude that the law is inherently tentative rather than fixed and certain in these areas. Yet we should not forget that we are talking to actors who have an interest in rendering the law ambiguous. We could equally talk to feminists or victims about rape, to trade unions about occupational health-and-safety offenses, to environmental groups about pollution, to prosecutors or regulatory agencies. These constituencies might just as actively struggle to project clarity into the law as accused offenders struggle to project ambiguity. It is an enormously valuable type of scholarship to study the struggle between those with an interest in clarifying and those with an interest in muddying the criminal-noncriminal distinction. My first concern is that we do not get carried away with the interpretive work being done on one side of that struggle that leads us to misperceive the criminal law as nothing but shifting sand. Rather, the product of that interpretive struggle is a core area of uncontroversially criminal conduct with a fringe of shifting sand whose width varies depending on the domain of law—wide with tax law, narrow with robbery.

To get at that uncontroversial core of the criminal law, one might do better than to tap the perceptions of either rapists on the defensive or feminists on the offensive. One might be more interested in the interpretive work of actors who are in a kind of Rawlsian original position—who do not bring a history of personal interest to their interpretive work, inclining them to want particular cases to be either ambiguous or clear. Where do we find such people, and how do we study them? This line of thought might lead us to a remarkable discovery—the judge and jury!

Now if we like, we can view the judge as a high priest of a capitalist legal order, with the jury under her spell. If this is the case, researchers may do better to bring together their own "people's courts" of lay jurors. Against this, however, is the view that the interpretive work that matters is that which constitutes the content of the law in practical institutional contexts, in the arenas where law is made. Again this leads us to discover the work of judges and juries, as well as legislators, as the more important and revealing interpreters of the law than either offenders or prosecutors, or even random citizens gathered to participate in a jury experiment.

There is, then, a contradiction in studying the views of those with an interest in problematizing the law in order to study ambiguities of legal definition. Interestingly, when we put offenders in more of an "original position" by asking them about how they interpret the delinquencies of their children rather than their own crimes, the evidence is that they disapprove of delinquency in a way similar to law-abiding parents, rather than excuse it as problematic (for example, West, 1982:49). The data we have point to overwhelming community consensus over the core areas of the criminal law (Rossi et al., 1974; Newman, 1976; Thomas, Cage, and Foster, 1976; Wright and Cox, 1967a, 1967b; Sellin and Wolfgang, 1964; Wilson and Brown, 1973; New South Wales Bureau of Crime Statistics and Research, 1974; Chilton and DeAmicis, 1975; Figlio, 1975; Hamilton and Rytina, 1980; Kutchinesky, 1973; Riedel, 1975; Rose and Prell, 1955; Wellford and Wiatrowski, 1975; Pontell et al., 1983; Rossi, Simpson, and Miller, 1985; but note the caveats of Miethe, 1982, 1984; and Cullen et al., 1985), a consensus for the most part shared by labeled criminals themselves.

The study of how offenders problematize the criminal law is important for a number of reasons. It helps illuminate how conflict over the content of the law unfolds; it engenders an appreciative stance toward the offender. All I am saying is that we should be wary of taking the offender's perception of the problematic nature of the law as definitive. The most valuable contribution of this style of research is not in the way it can undermine the possibility of explanetory theory, but in the way it can contribute toward it.

Most of us refrain from crime most of the time because to seize the criminal opportunity is unthinkable to us—we would not consider beginning to calculate the costs and benefits of committing murder or rape. Studying the views of criminals on how the law seems so problematic to them is one route to understanding why a particular crime was thinkable to them in a way it is not to others. Far from defeating the mission of explanatory theory building, interpretive sociology should be the most important tool of the theory builder's trade.

Alas, it has not been so used. Interpretive sociology in practice has tended to be obsessed with taking the side of the offender in a way that has contributed to the theoretical nihilism that is the state of criminology today.

We can ponder endlessly how disparate and multifarious are the causal histories of crimes with no face homogeneity; we can pile case upon case of offenders who contest the meaning of crime. Valuable as such data are, they should not persuade us one jot that general theories of crime are impossible. It may well be that general theories of crime are impossible, but the only way we will establish that is through repeated failures of attempts to build a general theory. As of the moment though, we cannot say that general theory has been tried by modern criminology and failed; rather, it has failed for the want of trying.

The paradox of the contemporary state of criminology is that we have allowed criminological theory to be paralyzed by developments that should have enhanced it—a growing appreciation of the ways that criminals render the criminal law problematic, and of the richness and diversity of the variables involved in causal histories of particular crimes.

After a great postwar blossoming of theoretical criminology—Sutherland and Cressey, Albert Cohen, Cloward and Ohlin, Short, Hirschi, and many others—one would be excused for thinking for the past two decades that the interactionist, phenomenological, Marxist revolutions had killed positive criminological theory stone dead. Happily, some adventurous spirits are now beginning to poke their heads above the trenches. Wilson and Herrnstein (1985) did so on the right side of the battlefield, and how we all relished finally having a target to shoot at. From the left we had a bold theoretical exposition by Colvin and Pauly (1983). They have not yet had their brains blown out, perhaps only because they don't come from Harvard.

The very fact that some theorists are beginning to scan the horizon rather than dig deeper into their familiar trench is encouraging for the future of criminology. I was also enormously encouraged by the advent of *Advances in Criminological Theory* and by the book edited by Bob Meier in 1985, *Theoretical Methods in Criminology,* which brought together some of criminology's brightest and best.

Charles Tittle's (1985) contribution to the latter volume is particularly relevant to the position I am developing here on the state of criminology. Tittle diagnoses the criminological malady of killing theories before they are given a chance to grow. Part of the fault lies within the theorists, who, Tittle says, either polemically limit their theory by presenting it as a counter to some mode of thought prevailing at the time the theory was written or present their work as some kind of final answer. Sutherland committed both these sins: he was not content to bill differential association as no more than "an important brick in an emerging edifice of general theory" (Tittle, 1985:113).

But the greater fault lies with the collective adversarial approach of criminology to theoretical work: "the social scientific community is more united in trying to prove the impossibility of general theory than it is in trying to construct one" (Tittle, 1985:116). So theories are viewed as the creations of individuals, who tend to defend them against a torrent of destructive criticism; neither the original theorist nor the critics are moved to reconstruct the theory in light of the data and argument generated by the debate.

The malady is of testing the original formulations of criminological theory, concluding they are wrong, and leaving it at that. What should we do instead? Tittle suggests that we move away from theories as immutable individual creations and seek to nurture a collective movement to build general theory. Under a healthy reciprocation between theory and research our initial interest should not be to show that "A causes B" in the original formulation of a theory is wrong, but to refine it, elaborate it, conditionalize, and add specificity to it. If the proposition is just plain wrong, we will discover that soon enough.

Unless we turn the culture of criminology around, the disincentives for clear, bold, manipulable formulations that make for testable prediction will continue to keep our heads down, protected by atheoretical descriptions that seem unexceptionable to everyone; by abstruse language that obscures tautology, nonprediction, and a failure to enter the symbolic world of offenders; and by methodological virtuosity that obscures the banality of just another kind of atheoretical description.

The present state of criminology is one of abject failure in its own terms. We can't say anything convincing to the community about the causes of crime; we can't prescribe policies that will work to reduce crime; we can't in all honesty say that societies spending more on criminological research get better criminal justice policies than those that spend little or nothing on criminology. Certainly we can say some important things about justice, but philosophers and jurisprudents were making a good fist of those points before ever a criminological research establishment was created.

We can also say some useful things about what does not work. Yet we have lacked the collective guts to undermine our institutional base by saying to policymakers that they really ought to save the taxpayers' money by spending less on the criminal justice system. At best we recommend occasional minor cuts in spending while acquiescing in the aggregate expansion of the system.

These occasional snippets of useful advice about things that don't work cannot sustain criminology in the long term. If that is all we are to continue doing, if we are no more than professional debunkers and cynics, then fifty years from now there will be far fewer people at the American Society of Criminology conference. The state can improve the health of people by spending public money on health services, and it can improve the housing of people by public spending on housing; scholars in these areas can say sensible, empirically informed things to governments about how these ends can be achieved. Criminology as a science has failed to put us in a position to say sensible, empirically informed things about protecting the community from crime.

When science fails us so utterly in this way, we must look to its fundamentals—its theory. The policy failure is a failure of explanation; we cannot solve it by retreating from the need to explain. The fruits of the atheoretical policy-oriented criminology of recent decades are not on the tree waiting to be plucked. The quick policy fixes are just not out there waiting to be discovered.

This is not to say that good policy analysis means identifying *the* general theory of crime and applying it to all and sundry policy problems. The reason economists do bad policy analysis so much of the time is because they do just that. No, the mission of criminology as a science should be to build theories of as general a scope as we can manage. Then, one would hope that policymakers would work through these theories as alternative frameworks for thinking about particular policy interventions. They might, for example, think dialectically about two general theories that are absolutely contradictory: the oppositions enfolded in the useful application of theory A today alert the policy analyst to switch intervention to a strategy more informed by theory B as the contradictions inherent in the application of theory A take effect. Perhaps a successful policy intervention of eliminating illegitimate opportunities of a certain sort will eventually sow the seeds of its own impotence by motivating criminals to actively create new illegitimate opportunities. Policy analysis is not a science; it is the art of "modeling through"! But criminology as a science has failed to supply policymakers with good models to model through with.

What we must do is some fundamental thinking about theoretical methods in criminology. We must abandon the theoretical nihilism that unites us against anyone who scans the horizon beyond their entrenched niches of expertise, nurture bold and general theory, and work cooperatively to build upon it rather than kill it in the womb.

References

Chilton, R., and J. DeAmicis. 1975. "Overcriminalization and the Measurement of Consensus." *Sociology and Social Research* 15:318–29.

Colvin, M., and J. Pauly. 1983. "A Critique of Criminology: Toward an Integrated Structural-Marxist Theory of Delinquency Production." *American Journal of Sociology* 89:513–51.

Cullen, F. T., B. G. Link, L. F. Travis, and J. F. Wonziak. 1985. "Consensus on Crime Seriousness: Empirical Reality or Methodological Artifact?" *Criminology* 23:99–118.

Figlio, R. M. 1975. "The Seriousness of Offenses: An Evaluation of Offenders and Non-Offenders." *Journal of Criminal Law and Criminology* 66:189–200.

Hamilton, V. L., and S. Rytina. 1980. "Social Consensus on Norms of

Justice: Should the Punishment Fit the Crime?'' *American Journal of Sociology* 85:1,117–44.

Kutchinesky, J. 1973. *Society and Deviance in Communist Poland: Attitudes towards Social Control*. Trans. M. Wilson. Leamington Spa, Warwickshire: Berg Publishers.

Meier, R. F., ed. 1985. *Theoretical Methods in Criminology*. Beverly Hills: Sage.

Miethe, T. D. 1982. ''Public Consensus on Crime Seriousness: Normative Structure or Methodological Artifact?'' *Criminology* 20:515–26.

———. 1984. ''Types of Consensus in Public Evaluations of Crime: An Illustration of Strategies for Measuring 'Consensus.' '' *Journal of Criminal Law and Criminology* 75:459–73.

Newman, G. 1976. *Comparative Deviance: Perception and Law in Six Cultures*. New York: Elsevier.

New South Wales Bureau of Crime Statistics and Research. 1974. *Crime, Correction and the Public*. Statistical Report 17. Sydney.

Pontell, H. N., C. Keenan, D. Granite, and G. Geis. 1983. ''White-Collar Crime Seriousness: Assessments by Police Chiefs and Regulatory Agency Investigators.'' *American Journal of Police* 3:1–16.

Riedel, M. 1975. ''Perceived Circumstances, Inferences of Intent and Judgments of Offense Seriousness.'' *Journal of Criminal Law and Criminology* 66:201–208.

Rose, A. M., and A. E. Prell. 1955. ''Does the Punishment Fit the Crime? A Study in Social Validation.'' *American Journal of Sociology* 61:247–59.

Rossi, P. H., J. E. Simpson, and J. L. Miller. 1985. ''Beyond Crime Seriousness: Fitting the Punishment to the Crime.'' *Journal of Quantitative Criminology* 1:59–90.

Rossi, P. H., E. Waite, C. E. Bose, and R. E. Berk. 1974. ''The Seriousness of Crimes: Normative Structure and Individual Differences.'' *American Sociological Review* 39:224–37.

Sellin, T., and M. Wolfgang. 1964. *The Measurement of Delinquency*. New York: Wiley.

Taylor, L. 1972. ''The Significance and Interpretation of Replies to Motivational Questions: The Case of Sex Offenders.'' *Sociology* 6:23–39.

Thomas, C. W., R. Cage, and S. Foster. 1976. ''Public Opinion on Criminal Law and Legal Sanctions: An Examination of Two Conceptual Models.'' *Journal of Criminal Law and Criminology* 67:110–16.

Tittle, C. R. 1985. ''The Assumption That General Theories Are Not Possible.'' In Meier 1985.

Wellford, C. F., and M. D. Wiatrowski. 1975. ''On the Measurement of Delinquency.'' *Journal of Criminal Law and Criminology* 66:175–88.

West, D. J. 1982. *Delinquency: Its Roots, Careers and Prospects*. London: Heinemann.

Wilson, J. Q., and R. Herrnstein. 1985. *Crime and Human Nature*. New York: Simon and Schuster.

Wilson, P. R., and J. W. Brown. 1973. *Crime and the Community*. Brisbane: University of Queensland Press.

Wright, D., and E. Cox. 1967a. "Religious Belief and Co-education in a Sample of 6th Form Boys and Girls." *British Journal of Social and Clinical Psychology* 9:23–31.

———. 1967b. "A Study of the Relationship between Moral Judgment and Religious Belief in a Sample of English Adolescents." *Journal of Social Psychology* 72:135–44.

9

One Perspective on the State of Criminology

Joan McCord

Four controversial issues lie at the core of criminology: definitions, the relationship between research strategies and the questions for which answers are sought, the assumption that psychological hedonism satisfactorily explains motivation, and the assumption that grand theory is good theory. These issues cut across domains of interest and theoretical persuasions. Yet they have been given, at best, peripheral attention. My purpose in discussing them is to bring these issues into focus as subjects worthy of discussion by criminologists.

Definitions

Philosophical consideration of language and its relation to empirical science began before Socrates. Recognizing the power of language in relation to reality, Parmenides wrote "That which can be spoken and thought . . . must be" (p. 345). Once a concept enters language, he noted, that to which it refers has existence. The force of language rests partly in the creation of concepts. We can look for an Oedipus complex (an unconscious desire on the part of a male to receive sexual gratification from his mother), lamda (a number representing the rate at which an individual commits crimes), and secondary reinforcements (a stimulus that serves as a reward because of its association with something that reduces action described as a drive) because these concepts have been referenced in language. None of these concepts can be defined denotatively. Perhaps it should be added, nor can numbers.

If we think of language as merely words, we pay too little attention to definitions and their implications. Definitions activate the machinery of enforcement. This becomes clear when we consider that they identify the illegal. They also control punishments, sometimes explicitly: "The penalty of criminal detention is not to be confused with *xingshi juliu,* by which is meant the pre-trial detention employed by the public security organs" (People's Republic of China, 1984: fn. p. 18).

Definitions also persuade. C. S. Stevenson (1944) thought this might account for the whole of moral judgements. Although he exaggerated, he captured what had been generally overlooked before he introduced the idea of "persuasive definition." To say of something that it is a "courageous act" is to stamp it with approval, to use a persuasive definition. When specific actions are defined as good, rather than bad, as right rather than wrong, as mature rather than immature, as normal rather than neurotic, or as heroic rather than stupid, we have shown the direction of social approval and added to the reasons for acting in a certain way.

Consider the concept of "moral maturity," masquerading under the guise of mere description. Moral maturity illustrates a persuasive definition. Scales correlated with age have been labeled as measures of stages in moral development.

As a feature of *language,* we should recognize that being mature is necessarily better than being immature. One can therefore mistakenly assume that scoring at a higher stage in the moral development scale is better than scoring at a lower stage.

But moral questions are not empirical questions, questions to be settled by counting ideas. G. E. Moore ([1903] 1959) claimed that any description of moral virtue fails to be a definition if it fails what he called "the Open Question." That question allows one to ask whether the thing referenced in the definition is itself good. So long as the question can be reasonably asked, we cannot settle a claim about morality by using that definition.

We ought to ask whether judgements made by older people are better than those made by younger ones. And so, we ought not *define* the former as at a higher stage of development. It may be true that both criminals and babies are hedonists. Nevertheless, moral judgements are not appropriately rated by maturity scales, and conceptual analysis alone should show that it is fallacious to conclude that criminals are at low stages of moral development.

Another thing that definitions do is identify as salient particular features of the environment. For example, the concept of a criminal career made salient the age at which criminal behavior begins, the frequency of criminal behavior, and variations in types of criminal activities. Because these features are tied to important events such as prison crowding, crime prediction, and crime prevention, the concept of criminal career is not trivial.

The concepts of "criminal career" and "career criminal" have sometimes been confused. A career criminal can be defined as a person whose illegal behavior plays the type of important role in his or her life that an occupation plays in the life of noncriminals. Career criminals typically are chronic offenders.

The link between definition and chronicity leads to what I will call "the continuum fallacy." The continuum fallacy is the fallacy of reasoning that because career criminals commit more crimes than other types of criminals, any group of criminals who commit more crimes than do others are career criminals. On the basis of this fallacy, the concept of career criminal turns up, in some studies, as meaning something like "those who committed the most crimes in the sample being studied." Confusing the more serious of community-based delinquents with career criminals does little to advance understanding of career criminals. We should not assume that knowledge about lesser offenders can be extended to knowledge about career criminals.

The continuum fallacy can be found also in studies of psychopaths, fallaciously identified as being the more aggressive, antisocial youths in a particular sample. A reasonable case can be made that psychopaths are not merely individuals with conduct-disorder problems (Hare, 1970; McCord, 1983). Studying nonpsychopathic people, however aggressive and antisocial they may be, will shed little light on the etiology of or cure for psychopathy.

A similar problem occurs in studies of the relationship between crime and alcoholism. Alcoholics are not merely individuals who drink heavily. Studies that mislabel heavy drinkers as alcoholics may lead to mistaken conclusions about the effects of alcohol. The effects of alcohol and its impact on crime could be different for alcoholics and nonalcoholics.

Research Strategies and Research Questions

The second controversial issue to be discussed is the relationship between research strategies and the questions for which answers are sought. Recently, lineups for a debate about research strategies have seemed to set the sides as being for or against longitudinal studies. This is unfortunate because the partisan arguments that follow may lead to expectations of too much—or too little—from such studies.

Some have argued that whatever can be learned from longitudinal studies can be as easily learned, for less money, using cross-sectional techniques. This is to claim that temporal order is irrelevant. Suppose that delinquents have rejecting mothers. Without longitudinal studies, there is no way to know whether delinquency causes rejection or rejection causes delinquency.

Longitudinal studies are necessary to learn many things; for example, longitudinal studies enable us to learn the temporal ordering among child aggressivity, parental rejection, and inconsistent discipline. The likelihood of designing a successful intervention strategy for working with families would be increased if we knew whether inconsistency was causal, consequential, or irrelevant to aggressivity. Similarly, longitudinal studies are necessary for learning the temporal ordering among educational problems, antisocial friendships, and delinquency.

Retrospective approaches to understanding events are dangerous because they can so easily be misleading. Once an event has occurred, the attempt to explain its occurrence should be suspect in regard to learning a causal story.

A priori rules govern explanations in such a way as to *require* biases. This can be illustrated by the following examples. Suppose Ellen was seen dancing down the street and an explanation was sought. An answer explaining that Ellen won the tennis match would be satisfactory as an explanation. But consider what happens when the same words are used to explain why Johnnie stole the watch. "Johnnie stole the watch because he won the tennis match" does not seem to provide a satisfactory explanation. At a minimum, it requires a further story.

The way in which winning the tennis match "explains" dancing and fails to explain a theft illustrates a difference between retrospective and prospective searches for causal explanations. After we know an outcome, explanations of it will be selective.

An explanation must include ingredients with the same evaluative status as that which will be explained. For this reason, a search through prior events to identify appropriate causal candidates cannot be trusted as a means to learn about the causes of crime. Conventions govern what will count as an appropriate explanation.

These conventions can be recognized in the breach. In the play "Crimes of the Heart," for example, Beth Henley used her knowledge of these conventions to set the scene as comic when Babe explained her mother's suicide: "She had a bad day. A real bad day." That explanation is funny only because bad days do not explain suicides.

True, temporal order does not prove causal connection. But mistakes about temporal order can produce false causal hypotheses. Longitudinal studies are indispensable to help get the temporal ordering right.

On the other hand, longitudinal studies are inappropriate for getting at questions of distribution. Better estimates of, say, the proportion of a city's residents who have committed crimes can be gained through multiwave, cross-sectional studies than by identifying a subset of residents for intensive study, especially if the subset will be restricted by such parameters as residential stability, parameters that may be related to crime.

Experimental longitudinal studies are probably the only means by which intervention can be given fair evaluation. Random assignments have been successfully used in family intervention (Rauh et al., 1988) and preschool programs (Berrueta-Clement et al., 1984), bail projects (Goldkamp and Gottfredson, 1985), and police studies (Sherman and Berk, 1984). They can and should be used more extensively.

Psychological Hedonism as Motivation

The third issue that deserves more attention than it has received pertains to the assumption that psychological hedonism satisfactorily explains motivation. Well-known criticisms of this Hobbesian position have been ignored (for example, Hume, [1777] 1960; Sidgwick, [1874] 1981). Only a handful of criminologists have considered the inadequacies of assuming that all people are always motivated by self-interest. In brief, these inadequacies include the following:

- Self-interest does not account for the appearance of benevolence, friendship, and love; for if the only real motive were self-love, particularity of preference would appear to have no source. (If we love or like someone else only because of the pleasure we get from friendship, it would not matter who we chose as lover or friend.)
- Self-love is unable to provide an account of happiness; if the only real desire were self-love, it would not be possible to have specific appetites, satisfaction of which sometimes produces happiness. (If we did not enjoy the opera or playing a good game of tennis, Don Carlo or serving an ace could not bring us pleasure.)
- Psychological hedonism allows no room for genuine moral judgements—and yet we make such judgements even about events far from us in time and place which could not be in our own self-interest. (If only self-interest could motivate, we would be unable to judge that American slavery was wrong.)
- Psychological hedonism allows no basis for distinguishing between altruism and egoism, though some people receive pleasure from benefiting others or promoting justice, while others receive more pleasure from being praised or made wealthy. (A motivational theory that cannot distinguish between those who help others and those who do not would fail to distinguish basic differences in action.)
- Psychological hedonism rests on circular reasoning; the assumption that a voluntary action must be motivated by a desire to do the action is confused with an assumption that a voluntary action must be motivated by a desire to benefit from the action. (Often, the only evidence for self-interest is the occurrence of the act for which a motive is being sought.)

If self-interest is not the only motivator, then rewards and punishments may be neither as important nor as straightforward in their effects as many believe. At a minimum, criminologists should be paying more attention to the evidence that suggests that pain can be rewarding (Solomon, 1980) and that rewards can act as disincentives (Lepper and Greene, 1978).

Grand Theory as Good Theory

And finally, the fourth controversial issue is the assumption that grand theory is good theory. Criminologists often seem to believe that a theory of crime must account for the existence of crime. "Strain," "social control," and "subcultural differences" have been hailed as the traditional theories of crime. These theories have been combined in various ways and tested by comparing them in terms of their ability to account for variance in either self-reported or officially recorded crime. Unfortunately, accounting for variance, though a cut above merely being significantly related to crime, has its own hazards in being dependent upon the sample chosen as well as on available measures and their collinearities.

Mistakenly, criminologists have often seemed to think that if criminology is to be a "real" science, it must have an overarching general theory. Yet scientific theories explain the trajectory of objects that have different mass, thrust, and surfaces; scientific theories explain how chemicals react and interact; scientific theories explain relationships among animals; scientific theories identify the cause and course of specific diseases. Such theories are parsimonious, predictive, and falsifiable. Yet these are not overarching general theories.

It seems to me that criminologists would do well to focus on using such models, providing theories that are less global (and perhaps less glamorous) than those that purport to explain crime completely.

This brief excursion around four controversial issues does not pretend to give a complete picture of the state of criminology. Perhaps, nevertheless, it raises issues and points of view that can contribute to the health of that state. If so, it has achieved its purpose.

References

Berrueta-Clement, J. R., L. J. Schweinhart, W. S. Barnett, A. S. Epstein, and D. P. Weikart. 1984. *Changed Lives: The Effects of the Perry*

Preschool Program on Youths Through Age 19. Ypsilanti, Michigan: The High Scope Press.

Goldkamp, J. S., and M. R. Gottfredson. 1985. *Policy Guidelines for Bail.* Philadelphia: Temple University Press.

Hare, R. D. 1970. *Psychopathy: Theory and Research.* New York: Wiley.

Hume, D. [1777] 1960. *An Enquiry Concerning the Principles of Morals.* La Salle, Ill.: Open Court.

Lepper, M. R. and D. Greene. 1978. *The Hidden Costs of Reward.* Hillsdale, N.J.: Lawrence Erlbaum.

McCord, J. 1983. "The Psychopath and Moral Development." In *Personality Theory, Moral Development, and Criminal Behavior,* edited by W. S. Laufer and J. M. Day, pp. 357–72. Lexington, Massachusetts: D. C. Heath.

Moore, G. E. [1903] 1959. *Principia Ethica.* Cambridge: Cambridge University Press.

Parmenides. *The Way of Truth.* From *The Presocratic Philosophers: A Critical History with a Selection of Texts,* by G. S. Kirk and J. E. Raven. 1962. Cambridge: Cambridge University Press.

People's Republic of China. 1984. *The Criminal Law and the Criminal Procedure Law of China.* Beijing: Foreign Languages Press.

Rauh, V. A., T. M. Achenbach, B. Nurcombe, C. T. Howell, and D. M. Teti. 1988. "Minimizing Adverse Effects of Low Birthweight: Four-Year Results of an Early Intervention Program." *Child Development* 59:544–53.

Sherman, L. W., and R. A. Berk. 1984. "The Specific Deterrent Effects of Arrest for Domestic Assault." *American Sociological Review* 49:261–72.

Sidgwick, H. [1874] 1981. "Pleasure and Desire." In *The Methods of Ethics.* Indianapolis: Hackett Publishing Co.

Solomon, R. L. 1980. "The Opponent-Process Theory of Acquired Motivation: The Costs of Pleasure and the Benefits of Pain." *American Psychologist* 35(8):691–712.

Stevenson, C. S. 1944. *Ethics and Language.* New Haven: Yale University Press.

Name Index

175

Subject Index